7.95

D1684293

WITHDRAWN

Kirtley Library
Columbia College
Columbia, Missouri 65216

Twayne's United States Authors Series

Sylvia E. Bowman, *Editor*

INDIANA UNIVERSITY

William James

WILLIAM JAMES

By BERNARD P. BRENNAN

TWAYNE PUBLISHERS
A DIVISION OF G. K. HALL & CO., BOSTON

Copyright © 1968 by Twayne Publishers, Inc.

All Rights Reserved

Library of Congress Catalog Card Number: 68-24290
ISBN: 0-8057-0408-6

MANUFACTURED IN THE UNITED STATES OF AMERICA BY
UNITED PRINTING SERVICES, INC.
NEW HAVEN, CONN.

To
EDWARD J. MORTOLA
President
Pace College

Contents

Chronology

1. The James Family — 13
2. The Man and His Career — 23
3. The Philosophic Enterprise: Pragmatism and Radical Empiricism — 44
4. Human Knowledge — 65
5. Truth and Certitude — 86
6. Philosophy of Religion — 98
7. The Universe — 126
8. The Moral Life of Man — 138
9. William James, Today and Tomorrow — 156

Notes and References — 159

Selected Bibliography — 170

Index — 173

Preface

WILLIAM JAMES, it was said, would impart life and charm to a treadmill; and he did impart a new life to philosophy, demanding changes far more profound than new formulations of the universe.

To convey to a beginner the principal angles of James's philosophical vision is the aim of this book. An introductory, systematic exposition of the philosophy of William James, Pragmatist and Radical Empiricist, is presented, with references to his achievements in psychology only in terms of their significance to his philosophy. Material from James's published and some previously unpublished writings has been organized around central philosophical problems: knowledge; truth and certitude; the philosophy of religion; the nature of the universe; the moral life of man.

James is presented as demanding profound changes in philosophic thinking; his "simplicity" is shown to have the profundity of a radical turning-point. His attacks upon abstractionism and scientism are presented as parts of his general demand that philosophical viewpoints take into account the total nature of the human person—emotional and volitional as well as intellectual. Against the dehumanizing effects of "vicious intellectualism" James calls for a genuine rationalism which includes faith and moral values.

In his advanced ethical thinking James foresaw the need to channel man's tremendous energies away from destructive expressions in war and emphasized the necessity to find its moral equivalent. He envisioned young persons, in particular, throwing their energies into a war against economic and social evils, a vision now realized in the Peace Corps.

For the contemporary individual, James's philosophy offers opportunities to discover high intelligibility in a variety of one's own personal experiences. It prepares one to deal fruitfully with his experiences, offering liberation from the closed mentality, and showing how to make an open-minded, imaginative use of experiences. It calls for faithfulness to one's own insights and demonstrates that all true knowledge must lead to action.

For suggestions and assistance in research and in the writing of this book, I am grateful to many persons at my college, but especially so to President Edward J. Mortola, President-emeritus and Mrs. Robert S. Pace, Dr. Thomas E. Sayles, Dr. John Waldman, Dr. Robert M. Dell, Dr. Bryce Thomas, Professor Jack Venema, Professor Muriel Shine, Dr. Gilbert Rubenstein, Professor Philip Waterson, Dr. Harold Lurier, Professor John Gibbon, Professor Irving Settel, Dr. Richard Gill, Mr. Henry Birnbaum, and Dr. Joseph Sinzer.

To Dr. Quentin Lauer, Dr. Robert Pollack, and Dr. John Flynn for their general encouragement to me to study and write and for introducing me to the study of William James I am especially indebted. For special assistance or encouragement, I must also thank Mrs. Peter Brennan, Mr. Vincent Garahan, Mr. H. Montgomery Hyde, Mrs. Joseph G. Shannon, Captain and Mrs. T. C. C. Vance, Reverend James Nelson, Reverend Bernard Brennan, Reverend and Mrs. J. Bond, Mr. Jacob Steinberg, and Miss Helen James. I am grateful to the members of the staff of the Houghton Library at Harvard, especially Mr. W. H. Bond, Miss Carolyn E. Jakeman, Miss Lynda H. Brown, and Miss Carol D. Goodman, for their assistance in the library, and to Mr. John S. R. James for his cordial interest in some of my James research.

Finally, permission to quote is gratefully acknowledged, as follows: to Holt, Rinehart and Winston, Inc. (William James, *The Principles of Psychology*); to Houghton Mifflin Company (Henry James, *Literary Remains;* William James, *Human Immortality*); to Charles Scribner's Sons (Henry James, Jr., *A Small Boy and Others;* Henry James, Jr., *Letters of Henry James, Jr.*); to Dodd, Mead and Company (Alice James, *Alice James: Her Brothers, Her Journal,* ed. A. R. Burr); to Little, Brown and Company (Perry, *The Thought and Character of William James*); and to Paul R. Reynolds, Inc. (Henry James, Jr., *The Letters of Henry James, Jr.*). For access to unpublished materials at the Houghton Library acknowledgment is also gratefully recorded.

BERNARD P. BRENNAN

Pace College
New York City
August 15, 1967

Chronology

1842 Born in New York City, January 11.
1857-　Boyhood studies and travels in Europe.
1860
1860-　At Newport, Rhode Island, studying painting with William
1861 Morris Hunt.
1861 First association with Harvard: studies in Lawrence Scientific School.
1863 Beginning of study of medicine, leading to the M.D. in 1869.
1865-　Biological studies with Louis Agassiz, on Brazilian ex-
1866 pedition.
1873-　Instructor in Anatomy and Physiology.
1876
1875 Beginning of instruction in psychology.
1876 Assistant Professor of Physiology.
1878 Marriage to Alice H. Gibbens.
1880 Assistant Professor of Psychology.
1885 Professor of Philosophy.
1890 Publication of *Principles of Psychology.*
1901-　*The Varieties of Religious Experience* presented as the
1902 Gifford Lectures.
1907 Publication of *Pragmatism.*
1908 *A Pluralistic Universe* presented as the Hibbert Lectures.
1910 Death at country home in Chocorua, New Hampshire, August 26.

CHAPTER *1*

The James Family

WILLIAM JAMES, born in New York City on January 11, 1842, was not, contrary to a general belief, a New Englander by birth or ancestry. His New England associations, so important in his life, were acquired in young manhood; and, although he shone brilliantly in the best New England circles, in Boston and Cambridge he remained an Irishman among the Brahmins. His ancestors were Irish and Scottish, associated with New York and New Jersey, the oldest branch of the American family being just short of a century old at the time of his birth. By that time, the family had made its mark and contributed richly to American life. It also had produced original, enterprising characters notable for their striking deeds and independent thoughts.

I Ancestors

The genealogy of the family can most conveniently be begun with the paternal grandfather of the philosopher, also called William James (1771-1832), and distinguished by the phrase "of Albany." An account of William of Albany is a logical starting point because of the huge fortune he bequeathed to succeeding generations and because of his staunch Presbyterian faith, which served both as an inspiration and as a point of departure for his descendents.

This William, son of William James (1736-1822) and Susan McCartney (1746-1824), emigrated from Ireland in 1789, leaving behind him in Bailieborough, County Cavan, his parents and two brothers; but nothing is known of William's ancestry, apart from a tradition in Ballyjamesduff which declares that the Jameses were of Norman origin. Once in America, William of

Albany applied himself to building a great fortune and to rearing a large family. He dedicated himself to the welfare of the church and joined the ranks of the old Dutch families of Albany in working for the development of the city and the state. The drive which William of Albany displayed in business and public life was matched by the energy which he devoted to his family life, in the course of which he fathered thirteen children by three wives, Elizabeth Tillman; Mary Ann Connolly, a devout Catholic, who maintained her faith in William's Presbyterian household; and Catherine Barber, the grandmother of the philosopher.[1]

This Catherine Barber James (1791-1859), "Grandma James," a great matriarch in Albany, was herself a noteworthy person. Her granddaughter Katherine Van Buren Wilson in 1920 recalled her vividly:

> You may say she had great strength of character—she was a wonderful woman. She brought up six sons and three daughters. Her unselfishness and goodness was known all over. They tell the story about her going to the door one day, and a poor beggar woman was there. Without hesitation she took off her flannel petticoat and gave it to her. Late in the evening she complained of being cold and her niece Miss Libby Courlay, who lived with her, upon examining why she was cold, said, "Why, Aunt James, you have no flannel petticoat on." "My goodness," said dear Grandma, "I forgot all about it. I gave it to a poor woman at the door!"
>
> The James record in Albany is beautiful. They were adored. Their hospitality and their generosity—indeed they were too generous, and I am *proud* I belong to them.[2]

Through Catherine Barber James, William the philosopher was related also to the Barber family, which contributed noted officers to the American cause in the Revolution. The first American Barber was Patrick (d. 1791), Catherine's grandfather, who emigrated from County Longford, Ireland, about 1750, finally settling in Orange County, New York State. His sons Francis, John, and William distinguished themselves in the Revolution. His son John was the father of Catherine Barber James.

Henry James, Sr. (1811-1882), was the fourth son of Catherine Barber James and William James of Albany. A distinguished religious and social philosopher, he profoundly influenced the

The James Family

life of his son William. Less prolific than his father, Henry Senior had four sons, William, the philosopher; Henry, Jr., the novelist; Garth Wilkinson and Robertson; and one daughter, Alice.

Henry Senior's wife was Mary Robertson Walsh (1810-1882); their marriage was performed on July 28, 1840, by the Mayor of New York in the bride's home at 18 Washington Square North. With this marriage Henry James Senior continued the Irish strain and added some Scotch. His wife, daughter of James Walsh and Elizabeth Robertson Walsh, was a descendant of Hugh Walsh of County Antrim and of Alexander Robertson of Scotland. On both sides of her family were colorful and public-spirited ancestors, but none more generous, probably, than Alexander Robertson (1733-1816). Of his generosity two examples are recorded:

> Alexander Robertson, Esq., merchant in this city, has made a donation to the Scotch Presbyterian Church of New York . . . for the noble purpose of charity; on which [donated lots] is to be erected a free school for the poor children of that congregation; all at his own private expense estimated in the whole to be in value £2000.[3]
>
> On his daughter's marriage to Peter McDougall, he [Alexander Robertson] sent to the sick in the Almshouse and the Debtors in jail, 150 loaves of bread, 300 lbs. of beef, 130 lbs. of cheese, 3 bbls. of strong ale, 3 bbls. of apples.[4]

Works of mercy performed in an amazing number of ways and splendid dedication to public welfare distinguish the Jameses. As far back as one can trace, these are hallmarks of the family.

II Henry James, Senior

That perceptive and lofty judge of character, Ralph Waldo Emerson, regarded Henry James, Sr., as a valued friend and described him as *the best man in the City of New York.* John Jay Chapman, with a flair for overstatement, declared that Henry Senior was the only decent man that ever lived in Massachusetts. Whatever may be the case, scholars of this century are relatively silent on James's work—much to the loss of this generation.

Though often thought of as a New Englander, Henry James, Sr., was one only by his own choice in later life and by acceptance by the finest people of Yankeedom. Born in Albany, he resided there and in New York City and abroad before he settled in Cambridge. As Anna Robeson Burr points out, "Mr. James never set foot in New England until his middle thirties, and retained many characteristics of an Irish descent in a New York setting. It is noticeable that while in New York he seemed rather Bostonian, yet once settled in Ashburton Place, he seemed too much of a New Yorker to find in Boston his spiritual home."[5]

After his graduation in 1830 from Union College, Henry studied at Princeton Theological Seminary from 1835 to 1837 in order to prepare for the ministry. But while there, his revolt against the doctrines of orthodox Calvinism came to a head; he withdrew from college and took the first of his many trips to Europe. In 1840 he married Mary Walsh, sister of his friend Hugh Walsh, also a former student at the seminary.

A genuine encounter with the senior Henry James's contributions to thought is unfortunately made difficult by the unusualness of his ideas, the eccentricities of his behavior, and the extravagances of his style. In his utterances he adopted the role of prophet and mystic, denouncing church and state. His code of behavior revolved around the conviction that respectability was the root of all evils. And his style was, as his son Henry observed, "too philosophic for life, and at the same time too living for thought."

This sage, mystic, and professed heretic devoted himself to a mission which remained clear and consistent throughout the course of his life. Every utterance, political, social, or religious, carried his conviction that *all men are equal because of the divinity which is in them.* Imperfections in individuals and in institutions he explained as due to a failure to recognize "the Lord's life in our nature."

Democracy, he believed, is to be cherished because it is the incarnation in social, political, and economic realms of that equality of men which has its prototype in the equality of all men before God. "Well, I take it," wrote James, "God is in one person quite as much as another. I don't see any difference in this respect between you [Julia A. Kellogg] and her, nor between you both and any drunken harlot that roams our streets. We come to speak of spiritual differences. He will be glorified in the spirit of the castaway, and crucified in yours and F. M.'s."[6]

The James Family

Democracy, he thought, was a preparation for that perfect society in which all narrow selfhoods would be dissolved in a universal brotherhood. Meanwhile, democracy does its preparatory work: "Its doctrine is one essentially of repentence or preparation, denouncing old abuses, revealing the iniquity of past legislation, exalting every valley of inequality, abasing every mountain of privilege, making straight whatsoever is crooked and smooth whatsoever is rough, so that all flesh from the smallest to the greatest shall experience the salvation of God."[7] In other words, the mission of democracy, like the mission of St. John the Baptist, prepares for the coming of the Lord—not now in the person of Christ but in the emergence of universal brotherhood.

In this perfect society man would attain that self-sufficiency and self-government which are his destiny because of his divine genesis. But in this society and in the truly democratic society which prepares its way, no man will seek to advance his own interests at the expense of other individuals. "I hate every man alike," wrote James, "who claims or accepts a personal consideration apart from the race, and see in him the veritable temper of antichrist."[8] In the spirit of utter unselfishness, man will seek not his individual salvation but universal salvation for all mankind: "I would take the risk of any amount of private damnation—what men call damnation—to help along for one moment the progress of God's justice on the earth. And I would abhor any amount of private salvation—what men call salvation—if I thought it an evidence of God's personal regard to me."[9]

To advance his philosophy, James published fourteen books, delivered innumerable lectures, engaged in endless discussions, and wrote hundreds of letters. In his private life he created an atmosphere for his family in line with his philosophy, starting with a union with his wife, which his son Robertson James described as "a perfect one both in heart and mind. No marriage could have been more perfect."[10] For his children he created an atmosphere of affection and stimulating freedom, devoting much time to developing their individuality and aiding the development of their talents.

His position in American thought was evaluated in 1928 by one admirer: "But nevertheless Henry James, the father of Henry the novelist, of William the philosopher, was a mystic of a profounder mind than Emerson, an accepter of his fellow men with a deeper understanding as Whitman, as fearless a scorner of the smug and conventional as Thoreau, and a more conscious plotter of an America that was no echo of an old rhapsody, but a New World indeed, than Poe ever dreamed of."[11] A much more modest account was given by William James, in publishing his father's literary remains; he felt that there was a great disproportion between his real greatness and the recognition accorded to him in his own time: "A man like my father, lighting on such a [anti-theological] time, is wholly out of his element and atmosphere, and is soon left stranded high and dry. His effectiveness as a missionary is null; and it is wonderful if his voice, crying in the wilderness and getting no echo, do not die away from sheer discouragement."[12]

Echoes there were, however muted and non-obvious though they be in the thought and character of this son William. For, as Ralph Barton Perry accurately noted, William resembled his father in personal flavor and genius, loving him with a filial love and an idealizing love: "He loved the kind of man his father was. And such being the fact he could not fail to grow like him, in his habits, his feelings, his appraisals, his attitudes."[13]

III *Brothers and Sister*

Of William James's brothers and sister, Henry James, Jr., Garth Wilkinson, Robertson, and Alice, only Henry, Jr., enjoyed what is known as worldly success. The others were excellent *men* in Henry James, Sr.'s, sense of that word; but only Henry, Jr., was a noted *person*. As a novelist, short story writer, and critic, Henry, Jr., enjoyed an international reputation in his own day, and today is ranked among the greatest of writers of fiction.

Garth Wilkinson James (1845-1883) and Robertson James (1846-1910) shared the extraordinary family life out of which the talented William and Henry, Jr., emerged to become famous men, but hardships and frustrations were their destiny. However, the short and simple annals of these younger brothers reveal heroic moral achievements worthy of the very best traditions of their family.

Before entering manhoods of hardship, they enjoyed boyhoods in the James household which Robertson James, in later

The James Family

years, described as having been "splendid." "The only thing to say of it," he wrote, "is that it was a beautiful and splendid childhood for any child to have had, and I remember it all now as full of indulgence and light and color and hardly a craving unsatisfied."[14] Garth's and Robertson's experiences in the James household and in the Sanborn School in Concord formed their minds and hearts in such a way that their most notable achievements in manhood arose out of their deep concern for Negro Americans. To the impassioned egalitarianism and abolitionist sentiments of their father was added the abolitionist fervor of Concord, especially that of Franklin B. Sanborn, headmaster of the Sanborn School.

In the summer of 1859 Henry, Sr., had placed Garth Wilkinson ("Wilky") and Robertson ("Bob") in the Sanborn School in Concord. Sanborn had been John Brown's ardent supporter and intimate friend. The atmosphere, surcharged with abolitionist sentiment, was raised to fever pitch by the news of John Brown's daring raid on Harper's Ferry. The wild reactions among the people of Concord engulfed young and old, masters and students:

> On October 16th came the Raid. At once Mr. Sanborn's situation became extremely critical. . . . A carriage and pair was got in readiness and by evening the schoolmaster was on his way to Quebec. . . . A peremptory note from Emerson brought Mr. Sanborn back before many weeks, where at various discussions followed as to the advisability of attempting to rescue John Brown before his trial, but the idea was abandoned as impractical. On the day of his execution, December 2, a "Martyr Service" was held in Concord which the whole community attended, in a state of the deepest, most shaking emotion . . . inevitably the two James boys, high-strung, imaginative adolescents, mentally developed beyond their years, present at these scenes, witnesses and sharers of these emotions, were affected by them for life.[15]

These experiences formed in Garth Wilkinson and Robertson a fervent resolve to aid the Negroes, and led not only to their enlistment in the Union Army in the Civil War but to their postwar project in Florida to assist the freedmen.

Following the Union victory, Garth and Robertson, though both were enfeebled as a result of sickness and wounds, asked their father to buy a plantation in Florida where they would prove that the freed Negroes could perform as satisfactory laborers without the constraints of slavery. Southerners had no faith in free Negro labor, and there was a need to demonstrate that they were wrong. The project succeeded in that particular respect, as Garth reported in a letter to his father:

> We came down and settled in a region where many of the inhabitants had never seen a Yankee. . . . None of them had faith in Negro labor, all of them in fact jeered at the thought of any man being able to keep them one week together. We started our farm, got together our hands. . . . Our hands began to work; and in two months got through an immense amount of labor . . . in less than a month most of the planters about us were hiring Negroes themselves and starting their own farms again . . . we have fully vindicated the principle we started on, that the freed Negro under decent and just treatment can be worked to profit to employer and employee.[16]

Alice James (1848-1892), an invalid most of her life, enjoyed her role as the cherished "only sister." She too recorded, two years before her death, as she read a collection of their letters, the happy homelife created by her mother and father: "It seems now incredible to me that I should have drank [sic] as a matter of course at that ever springing fountain of responsive love, and bathed all unconscious in that flood of human tenderness. Their letters are made up of the daily events of their pure, simple lives, with souls unruffled by the ways of men. . . . What a beautiful picture do they make for the thoughts of their children to dwell upon."[17]

Alice James's last years were spent in England in order to be near her bachelor brother, Henry, Jr., whose career was a source of delight to her. The rich record of these years, preserved in her *Journal*, reveals her interest in the welfare of the poor, her contempt for the English aristocracy, her concern for Irish freedom, her interest in old friends and family, and her gratitude to those who attempted to make her life bearable. The *Journal* also reveals, as her brother Henry pointed out, a moral and personal picture: "It is heroic in its individuality, its independence—its face-to-face with the universe for and by herself—and the beauty and eloquence with which she often expresses this, let alone the

The James Family

rich irony and humour, constitute a new claim for family renown."[18]

Warmly devoted to Alice and to his brothers and parents, Henry James, Jr., was in the uncomfortable position of one who did not feel at home in his own native land. Where William's democracy, Pragmatism, and pluralism, for example, fitted in comfortably with the American atmosphere, Henry's love of old feudal families, old castles, picturesque cities, and formal manners clashed with the newness and rawness of America and found fulfillment only in the Old World.

As a boy, Henry fitted into the role of being a younger brother to extroverted William with some difficulty, but with a devotion and good will that lasted throughout a lifetime. During boyhood days in New York, William is said to have spurned with typical big-brother scorn the company of Henry on one occasion, saying, "I play with boys who curse and swear!" Henry's devotion to his brother William in due time grew to include Alice, William's wife, and their children, to whom the great novelist was beloved "Uncle Henry."

Professionally, Henry and William shared a profound interest in the conduct of human beings. For William, this interest led to the open-minded, enthusiastic interest in all data concerning man, especially regarding psychology, ethics, and the theory of knowledge. For Henry, there developed the deep interest in the finest works of man—cities, churches, and the works of art, as preserved in his travel essays—and a profound understanding of social structures and of the feelings of individuals, in his short stories and novels. The philosopher had a novelist's taste for concreteness and variety, and the novelist brother had a psychologist's power in discerning the subtlest nuances of conduct and thought.

With all their shared interests and experiences, William and Henry, despite the best of good will, never succeeded in fully understanding each other's work. For Henry's brotherly claim that he, Henry, was a pragmatist, there is no substantiating evidence; and William confessed to being unable to "appreciate" many of Henry's works. The possibility of tension because of their differences of taste and temperament worried each of them, and each brother wondered how he might be disturbing to the other. On this point William was especially sensitive: "He and I are so utterly different in all our observances and springs of action, that we can't rightly judge each other. I even feel great shrinking from urging him to pay us a visit, fearing it might yield him out little besides painful shocks—and, after all, what besides pain and shock *is* the right reaction for anyone to make upon our [American] vocalization and pronounciation? . . . He is at bottom a very tender-hearted and generous being!"[19] Henry, also aware of the gap between them, even as late as 1905 expressed the hope that William would read none of his writings:

> . . . I'm always sorry when I hear of your reading anything of mine, and always hope you won't—you seem to me so constitutionally unable to "enjoy" it, and so condemned to look at it from a point of view remotely alien to mine in writing it, and to the condition out of which, as mine, it has inevitably sprung—so that all the intentions that have been its main reason for being (with me) appear even to assume that the life, the elements forming its subject-matter, deviate from felicity in not having an impossible analogy with the life of Cambridge. I see nowhere about me done or dreamed of the things that alone for me constitute the interest of the doing of the novel—and yet it is in a sacrifice of them on their very own ground that the thing you suggest to me evidently consists. It shows how far apart and to what different ends we have to work out (very naturally—and properly!) our respective intellectual ends.[20]

CHAPTER 2

The Man and His Career

IN REPORTS regarding the character and personality of William James certain words are repeated over and over. Observers agree in describing James as tolerant, manly, liberal, romantic, impetuous, mystical, generous, anti-traditionalistic, sensitive, brilliant, kind, eloquent. They see him as cosmopolitan, urbane, open-minded, optimistic, anti-fatalistic, energetic, humanistic, and sociable. Bertrand Russell saw in him democratic feelings and complete naturalness, combined with the personal distinction of a "natural aristocrat."[1]

But perhaps the most generally significant feature of James's being was his hunger for "feeling at home"—a desire for spiritual, social, and material surroundings in which his Socrates-like genius for friendships could unfold. In philosophy he demanded a universe of such a nature that it could be man's great *socius*, man's true friend and true home. In his private life his genius for loving relationships made his dwellings in Cambridge and in New Hampshire true homes for his family and havens for his friends and students; his intense personal interests in his colleagues and students made Harvard another home; his international friendships, bringing him warmly into the lives of many kinds of people, made the larger world of humanity a Jamesian hearth; and his profound at-home feeling with the great world of nature made him as much at home in nature as Henry Thoreau or William Wordsworth. His universal friendliness, extending even to the "spirit world," led him to years of dedicated psychic research. Including all nations in his empathy, he energetically battled against the forces of imperialism and militarism.

Although it was relatively late in his life when James formally became a philosopher, his entire life was filled with activities which prepared him for philosophy. His experiences as the son of Henry James, Sr., as an art student and a medical student, as a physiologist and psychologist, along with his own profound wrestling with despair and problems of human freedom, idealism, and the mystery of evil, provided the personal matrix in which he examined the philosophy of others and developed his own original philosophy. This philosophy was well developed by the time he became professor of philosophy at Harvard. He was destined to become, as Alfred North Whitehead said, "one of the greatest philosophic minds of all time."[2]

I *In His Father's Home*

The future philosopher was off to an auspicious start when his father invited Emerson upstairs "to admire and give his blessing to the lately-born babe who was to become the second American William James."[3] This presentation, which occurred within a short time after William's birth on January 9, 1842, provides an insight into the intellectual quality of the household in which he would grow up. And the fact that the birth and presentation took place in the Astor House, the leading hotel in New York, indicates the wandering propensities of Henry Senior, who found little attraction in a permanent abode—until years later when he settled in Boston and Cambridge.

Henry Senior, having abandoned his early plans for a career in the ministry, found other professions incompatible; and, being financially independent, he became a professional student: he devoted himself to learning and to propagating his views—and to educating his children. This education was designed to minimize the influences of institutions and grim traditions and to develop talents and interests with the greatest amount of freedom. To pursue educational opportunities, the family moved from New York, to Europe, to Newport, to Boston and to Cambridge; and individual members made independent excursions here and there, for example, William to Brazil to study under Agassiz.

William could not have been expected to learn much from his first European trip, which took place before his second birthday; on returning from Europe, the Jameses resided briefly in Albany, and then settled in New York for ten years. During these years William and his brother Henry, Jr., shared an odd assortment of educational experiences in various schools and the perhaps more valuable experiences of life in a great city.

The New York of those days, vividly presented in the reminiscences of young Henry,[4] was still homogeneous but had cosmopolitan elements; and Henry and William enjoyed the city with youthful gusto. As Henry recalled, they enjoyed Broadway, "the feature and the artery, the joy and the adventure of one's childhood"; they suffered on Saturdays on Wall Street in "the torture chamber of Dr. Parkhurst, our tremendously respectable dentist, who was so old and so empurpled and so polite, in his stock and dress-coat and dark and glossy wig, that he had been our mother's and our aunt's haunting fear in *their* youth as well";[5] they were rewarded with trips to Taylor's or Thompson's for dishes of ice cream, "deemed sovereign for sore mouths, deemed sovereign in fact, through all our infancy, for everything." With their father, they visited the office of the New York *Tribune*, "a wonderful world indeed, with strange steepnesses and machineries and noises and hurrying bare-armed, bright-eyed men, and amid the agitation clever, easy, kindly, jocular, partly undressed gentlemen (it was always July or August) some of whom I knew at home. . . ."[6]

And there was the social life of New York, with innumerable visiting cousins, and Emerson and other noted men conversing in the parlor. The manners of the time were good, and Henry recalled "the note of sovereign ease of all the young persons with whom we grew up."[7] The James children in all this were trained to be democrats: "we were bred in horror of *conscious* propriety, of what my father was fond of calling 'flagrant' morality."[8]

In line with Henry, Senior's, feelings against all churches (organized ecclesiasticisms, he called them), the family had no regular church connection; but there was ample religious instruction at home. When his children desired to explain to their friends why they didn't belong to a church, the father declared "that we could plead nothing less than the whole privilege of Christendom and that there was no communion, even that of the Catholics, even that of the Jews, even that of the Swedenborgians, from which we need find ourselves excluded."[9]

A somewhat similar situation existed with respect to education. Just as their father was "all for" religion but indifferent or hostile to churches, so he was "all for" education but dubious about the merits of schools. His children were transferred from one school to another; disappointed with education in New York, Henry, Senior, thought of going to Europe. Finally, in 1849, the family, now consisting of four sons, mother, and father, set off for education in Europe. Henry explained his motives to Emerson: ". . . looking upon our four stout boys, who have no play-room within doors, and import shocking bad manners from the street, with much pity, we gravely ponder whether it would not be better to go abroad for a few years with them, allowing them to absorb French and German and get a better sensuous education than they are likely to get here."[10]

But another motive, undoubtedly, was at work: his determination to keep his family free from "stagnant isolation from the race." Henry James Sr.'s own boyhood in Albany had been, to his regret, isolated and stagnant: "Our family righteousness," he recalled, "had as little felt relation to the public life of the world, as little connection with the common hopes and fears of mankind, as the number and form of the rooms we inhabited; and we contentedly lived the same life of stagnant isolation from the race which the great mass of our modern families live, its surface never dimpled by anything but the duties and courtesies we owed our private friends and acquaintances."[11]

Educational odysseys in 1843-44, 1855-58, and 1859-60 took the family to England, France, and Switzerland. The boys were enrolled in various schools and studied privately with a number of tutors. They visited museums and theaters; they lived with European families and resided in the London of Victoria and in the Paris of Napoleon III. They got a rich "sensuous education" and broke for all time the bonds of "stagnant isolation from the race." The European experiences were a success, and the Jameses returned home so that William could study art with William Morris Hunt.

II *Art and Science*

Henry, Junior, in his reminiscences of boyhood, recalled the most characteristic image of William as "drawing, always drawing, especially under the lamp-light of the Fourteenth Street back parlour."[12] In Europe, young William had continued to draw and sketch, and he had spent hours admiring beautiful paintings

The Man and His Career

in the museums. In 1860 he decided to try being a painter: "I shall know in a year or two," he wrote, "whether I am made to be one. If not, it will be easy to retreat. There's nothing in the world so despicable as a bad artist."[13] The family returned from Europe and settled in 1860 in Newport, near the studio of William Morris Hunt, and William worked each day in Hunt's studio. But within a year the study of art was abandoned. In the fall of 1861, William made his first connection with Harvard University by registering in the Lawrence Scientific School, hoping to find his vocation there.

His scientific studies proved more congenial, but he remained uncertain about his vocation. Physical frailty precluded enlistment to fight in the Civil War, which had just erupted. While his two younger brothers went to war, William took up his studies, first concentrating on chemistry.

His teacher of chemistry, Charles William Eliot, later president of Harvard, recorded his impressions of James as a student: "James was a very interesting and agreeable pupil, but was not wholly devoted to the study of chemistry. . . . His excursions into other sciences and realms of thought were not infrequent. . . . His tendency to the study of physiology had appeared clearly during his two years in the Department of Chemistry. . . ."[14]

When William James later moved over to the study of physiology, he came under the influence of Professor Jeffries Wyman, a scientist noted for his extreme caution, accuracy, and "complete and simple devotion to objective truth." In the five years during which young James studied under him, Wyman ". . . contributed greatly to the forming of that scientific conscience which exercised a constant censorship upon James's speculative profligacy." To Wyman, James also was indebted for his competence on the problem of evolution—and for his "ideal of scientific purity."[15]

The other Harvard teacher who influenced him deeply was the great Louis Agassiz, whom James later described as being ". . . one of those folio copies of mankind, like Linnaeus and Cuvier."[16] From Agassiz he learned to admire the concrete as opposed to the abstract, to prize facts, and to distrust theories: ". . . the hours I spent with Agassiz," he wrote in 1898, "so taught me the difference between all possible abstractionists and all livers in the light of the world's concrete fulness, that I have never been able to forget it. Both kinds of minds have their place in the infinite design, but there can be no question as to which kind lies nearer to the divine type of thinking."[17]

Agassiz not only offered training in observation and thinking but also, by the force of his titanic personality, moulded his students into genuine scientists. He had a remarkable faith in himself and his work, and he appealed strongly to James, who was still seeking *his* role in life. Decades later, at the close of the century, the memory of Agassiz's faith still inspired James: "If ever a person lived by faith, he did. When a boy of twenty, with an allowance of two hundred and fifty dollars a year, he maintained an artist attached to his employ, a custom which never afterwards was departed from,—except when he maintained two or three."[18]

James's scientific interests brought him next to the study of medicine. On February 21, 1864, he wrote, "I embraced the medical profession a couple of months ago. My first impressions are that there is much humbug therein. . . ."[19] These medical studies were interrupted by James's participation in the Thayer Expedition to Brazil, led by Agassiz. After a year's absence (March, 1865, to March, 1866), he returned to Harvard Medical School; and in 1869 he passed his examination for the M.D., with no difficulty except for midwifery, which, he said, "gave me some embarrassment."[20] In the meanwhile, he had been traveling in Europe and had been plagued with ill health and acute depression. He had continued his interest in science and had been getting more and more interested in philosophic questions. He had been reading Immanuel Kant and Charles Renouvier, and his depression had deepened his interest in philosophic problems.

Instead of practicing medicine after he had received his degree, James continued as a student. Physiology became his major interest, but ill health forced him to drop out for a year and a half, during which he traveled and studied in Germany (1867-1868).

For several years James remained too ill to follow any career or systematic study; he was well by 1872, and full of enthusiasm. He was ready to take up a profession. In August, 1872, he was appointed Instructor in Physiology at Harvard College, beginning a service to the university which he continued until 1907. In 1875 he gave a graduate course entitled "The Relations be-

The Man and His Career

tween Physiology and Psychology"; he was moving rapidly toward specializing in psychology. In 1876 he organized a psychological laboratory; in 1877 his course on psysiological psychology was transferred to the Department of Philosophy and called "Psychology." In 1878, he was well removed from physiology, for in June he signed a contract to write the text on psychology which appeared in 1890 as *Principles of Psychology*.

III Cambridge: Family and Harvard

William James's life moved ahead in other respects also in a very satisfactory manner. On July 10, 1878, he was married in Boston to Alice Howe Gibbens, the daughter of Daniel Lewis Gibbens, M.D., and Eliza Putman Webb. Mrs. James was the great-great-granddaughter of "Fitch Gebbons" (Fitzgibbons?) who had emigrated to Massachusetts from County Waterford, Ireland, about 1750.[21]

This marriage was, as their son Henry observed, "a marriage in the rarest and fullest sense." "No mere devotion could have achieved the skill and care with which his wife understood and helped him. Family duties and responsibilities, often grave and worrisome enough, weighed lightly in the balance against the tranquility and confidence that his new domesticity brought him."[22] The household of William James must have been in many ways like the happy home in which he had grown up. With his four boys and his girl; his comfortable Cambridge home within walking distance of his classes; his country home at Chocorua, New Hampshire, rich in White Mountains scenery; and his solicitous wife, Professor James was truly "at home."

With his marriage in 1878 and his promotion in 1876 to an assistant professorship, James was established for life in an ideally suited and stimulating set of relationships. His wife was "a remarkable woman in her own right, distinguished in beauty, wit, and character";[23] and Harvard University, surcharged with vitality, gave him endless opportunities for research, writing, and teaching.

From his first teaching assignment down through the years to his retirement, the Harvard environment encouraged James's best efforts. His appointment to teach philosophy he regarded as a "perfect godsend," and he cherished every association with the university. When he traveled, he invariably compared foreign universities with his own, and in the comparison Harvard came out ahead with reference to teaching and cosmopolitanism. Writing from Paris to his brother Henry in 1882, he declared, "Nowhere did I see a university which seems to do for *all* its students anything like what Harvard does. Our methods throughout are better. It is only in the select 'Seminaria' (private classes) that a few German students making researches with the professor gain something from him personally which his genius alone can give. I certainly got a most distinct impression of my own *information* in regard to *modern* philosophic matters being broader than of any one I met, and our Harvard post of observation being more cosmopolitan."[24]

Twenty-five years later, when the LL.D. was conferred on him, James, speaking at the Harvard Commencement Dinner, explained the meaning of "the true Harvard," which had been his professional home for so many years. He saw Harvard as many things in one—"a school, a forcing house for thought, and also a social club."[25] But, observing that any college can foster "club loyalty," he declared, "the only rational ground for pre-eminent admiration of any single college would be its pre-eminent spiritual tone. But to be a college man in the mere clubhouse sense—I care not of what college—affords no guarantee of real superiority in spiritual tone."[26] The inner spiritual Harvard had pre-eminent spiritual tone because of her "persistently atomistic constitution, . . . her tolerance of exceptionality and eccentricity, . . . her devotion to the principles of individual vocation and choice":[27]

> The true Church was always the invisible Church. The true Harvard is the invisible Harvard in the souls of her more truth-seeking and independent and often very solitary sons. . . . The university most worthy of rational admiration is that one in which your lonely thinker can feel himself least lonely, most positively furthered, and most richly fed. . . . But as a nursery for independent and lonely thinkers I do believe that Harvard is still in the van.[28]

Harvard students enjoyed informal exchanges with William James in classes and in his home. Some of them became famous, and oddly enough two of the most famous were among the very small number of people whom James actively disliked: Theodore Roosevelt and George Santayana. The poorer and humbler students attracted him strongly; among this number was the Negro W. E. B. Du Bois.

IV A Philosopher's Friendships

William James had very few genuine disciples, but he engaged a large number of friends in a lifelong philosophical dialogue. On both sides of the Atlantic he sought friendships, which he nourished with letters, exchanges of photographs, hospitality, favors, and every courtesy natural to a genuinely sociable man. These friends included students, companions of his children, relatives of all degrees (including his beloved mother-in-law), neighbors, jurists, fellow mountain-climbing enthusiasts, reformers, colleagues, psychic researchers, and the leading psychologists, physiologists, and philosophers of his day. To all he imparted, by his cheerfulness, kindness, and faith, some of his philosophic angle of vision. His communications with women were brightened by gallantry—a solemn gallantry toward the eighty-year-old widowed Mrs. Louis Agassiz, President of Radcliffe College, and a playful gallantry toward Miss Pauline Goldmark of his mountain-climbing set in the Adirondacks.

In his associations with philosophers and psychologists, human interest kept pace with the exchange of ideas. James sought out personal contacts with the most creative thinkers and tried to see them in person; he observed them in their lecture halls and laboratories, and visited them in their homes. Having established a friendship, James mailed books, letters, and articles; he participated in exchanging visiting professorships and invitations to international congresses; he provided encouragement, criticism, and guidance to novices and internationally recognized experts. Italians were told of William James by Giovanni Papini; Americans, through James, became aware of the greatness of Henri Bergson; Harvard, through James's recommendations, sought out Hugo Münsterberg for its faculty.

The great international "forum" of James's friends included both friends and foes of his own viewpoints. He eagerly sought out discussions with Josiah Royce, for example, who represented at Harvard the antithesis of James's philosophy; he responded with delight to the thoughts of Henri Bergson, whose philosophical work, like his own, was grounded in concrete experience. To friend and foe he acknowledged intellectual debts—but sometimes all too generously. He admired those who had a capacity for friendship, and his description of persons with such a capacity applies well to himself: " '. . . certain persons do exist with an enormous capacity for friendship and for taking delight in other people's lives; and . . . such persons know more of the truth than if their hearts were not so big. The vice of ordinary affection . . . is not its intensity, but its exclusions and its jealousies."[29]

For James, philosophizing with a group of friends was a delightful and creative complement to solitary study in the library. As early as the 1870's this dialoguing had evolved into "The Metaphysical Club," recalled poignantly years later by Charles Sanders Peirce:

> It was in the early seventies that a knot of us young men in Old Cambridge, calling ourselves, half-ironically, half-defiantly, "The Metaphysical Club," for agnosticism was then riding its high horse, and was frowning superbly on all metaphysics—used to meet, sometimes in my study, sometimes in that of William James. It may be that some of our old-time confederates would to-day not care to have such wild-oats-sowings made public, though there was nothing but boiled oats, milk, and sugar in the mess. Mr. Justice Holmes, however, will not, I believe, take it ill that we are proud to remember his membership. . . . Chauncy Wright, something of a philosophic celebrity in those days, was never absent from our meetings. . . . John Fiske and, more rarely, Francis Ellingwood Abbot, were sometimes present, lending their countenances to the spirit of our endeavors, while holding aloof from any assent of their success.[30]

Chauncey Wright was a philosophic dialoguer with both James and his father, and enjoyed intimate acquaintance with both generations of the James family. But to both William and Henry, Senior, Wright was a philosophical adversary whose Positivism was strongly repugnant to the religious and metaphysical temperaments of the Jameses. As early as the mid-1870's William made notes entitled "Against Nihilism" to refute Wright's Positivistic views. By this date James had arrived at his conviction that Positivists were led to their position by personal, subjective interests fully as much as were religious persons or metaphysicians. "He attributed Wright's intellectual parsimoniousness to a 'defect in the active or impulsive part of his nature,' and designed his own study of the 'motives which lead men to philosophize' as a proof that positivism was both narrow and arbitrary."[31]

Another intimate friend of both Henry, Senior, and William was Charles S. Peirce, who was admitted to the family circle and took a keen interest in the views of the elder Henry. William and Peirce saw in each other excellence of character and genuine philosophic powers. James referred to Peirce as an *original man*, "willing and able to devote the powers of his life to logic and metaphysics."[32] Peirce believed James was as perfect a lover of the truth as it is possible for a man to be: "After studying William James on the intellectual side for half a century . . . I must testify that I believe him to be, and always to have been during my acquaintance with him about as perfect a lover of the truth as it is possible for a man to be; and I do not believe there is any definite limit to man's capacity for loving the truth. . . ."[33]

In 1906, in his famous lectures on Pragmatism, James carefully explained that the word *Pragmatism*, as he was using it, was "first introduced into philosophy by Mr. Charles Peirce in 1878." Having briefly explained the meaning of "Pragmatism," James said: "This is the principle of Peirce, the principle of pragmatism. It lay entirely unnoticed by anyone for twenty years, until I, in an address before Professor Howison's philosophical union at the University of California, brought it forward again and made a special application of it to religion. By that date (1898) the times seemed ripe for its reception. The word 'pragmatism' spread, and at present it fairly spots the pages of the philosophic journals."[34]

As James developed his meanings of Pragmatism (see Chapter III), Peirce, however, found them increasingly at variance with his own meanings. With the adoption of the word by F. C. S. Schiller and the "literary journals," Peirce decided, good-naturedly, to abandon "pragmatism": "So then, the writer, finding his bantling 'pragmatism' so promoted, feels that it is time to kiss his child good-by and relinquish it to its higher destiny; while to serve the precise purpose of expressing the original definition, he begs to announce the birth of the word 'pragmaticism,' which is ugly enough to be safe from kidnappers."[35]

One of the most crucial influences upon James's intellectual development was that of Charles Renouvier, the French philosopher, who rescued James from his commitment to philosophical determinism and from the spiritual, emotional, and intellectual depression occasioned by that determinism. The reading, in 1870, of Renouvier's *Psychologie rationnelle*, with its doctrine of freedom, solved a crisis in James's life, giving him at one and the same time, "health, courage, and insight."[36] In 1873, James attributed his improved outlook and activity to the reading of Renouvier (and of Wordsworth);[37] and in the last decade of his life, James continued to affirm his indebtedness to Renouvier: "I think that Renvouvier made mistakes, and I find his whole philosophic manner and apparatus too scholastic. But he was one of the greatest of philosophic characters, and but for the decisive impression made on me in the seventies by his masterly advocacy of pluralism, I might never have got free from the monistic superstition under which I grew up."[38]

Although James was to come to criticize Renouvier for becoming too "classical," systematic, and traditional, the influence of Renouvier on James was profound and permanent. Both agreed on the reality and priority of the *moral* world, and each developed a metaphysics in which the moral life of man had the highest significance. In the development of James's metaphysics, his pluralism was indebted to Renouvier's argument "that the world may *compose* a whole without being determined by it . . . that unity should not predetermine the many."[39]

Another contemporary philosopher whom James greatly admired was the Englishman Shadworth Hodgson. James ranked him with Renouvier as one of the two foremost contemporary philosophers and once regarded him as "the wealthiest mine of thought" he had ever met.[40] But in the course of philosophical development, James and Hodgson moved to opposite points of view on basic questions. By 1885, James found Hodgson's article on free will leaving "entirely untouched what seems to me the only living issue involved." "The paper," he said, "is an exquisite piece of literary goldsmith's work, . . . but it hangs in the air of speculation and touches not the earth of life. . . ."[41] In particular, James was deeply distressed when Hodgson proclaimed a deterministic world-view and tried at the same time to save some kind of moral freedom. "What a mockery then seems your distinction between determination and compulsion, between passivity and an 'activity' every minutest feature of which is pre-appointed...!"[42]

Such a disappointment was out of the question in James's relationships with Josiah Royce. From the very beginning their philosophical positions were clearly antithetical; Royce, being a Hegelian and an Absolute Idealist, could hardly have been further away from James's Pragmatism and Empiricism. Yet their personal and professional relationships were always most cordial. It was James who gave the strongest encouragement to Royce to become a professional philosopher, and it was he who prepared the way for Royce's appointment at Harvard.[43] It was James who recommended Royce as "a man from whom nothing is too great to expect,"[44] and the open-minded James eagerly examined Royce's "brand-new arguments for Absolute Idealism."[45]

James made a full study of Royce's arguments for Absolute Idealism, reading his books and, in the course of their thirty years as colleagues, exchanging ideas in letters and conversations. But, as always, James found that every form of monism denied man's desire for moral freedom, failed to explain finitude or evil, and contradicted experience. The objections against the monism of Spinoza and Hegel remained valid against Royce's Absolute Idealism. After much brooding over Royce's arguments, James concluded that Royce's system was a "light production": "The book [*The World and the Individual*] consolidates an impression which I have never before got except by glimpses, that Royce's system is through and through to be classed as a light production. It is a charming, romantic sketch; and it is only by handling it after the manner of a sketch, keeping it within sketch technique that R. can make it very impressive. In the few places where he tries to grip and reason close, the effect is rather disastrous."[46]

James saw Royce's failure to pay attention *to experience* as his fundamental error. Instead of accepting the concrete data of experience, wherein things are *dependent* in one respect and *independent* in another, Royce rejected pluralism and affirmed the priority of the whole as against the parts. Instead of deriving the unity of the world from the sum of its parts as James did, Royce affirmed the primal unity of all being—earning from James the accusation of abstractionism and vagueness. James believed that Royce's monism made careless use of abstractions and indiscriminately confused experience and dialectic, and he concluded in 1899 that "looseness of thought" was Royce's "essential element":

> Since teaching the "Conception of God," I have come to perceive what I didn't trust myself to believe before, that looseness of thought is R's *essential* element. He *wants* it. There isn't a tight joint in his system; not one. And yet I thought that a mind that could talk me blind and black and numb on mathematics and logic, and whose favorite recreation is works on those subjects, must necessarily conceal closeness and exactitudes of ratiocination that I hadn't the wit to find out. But no! he is the Rubens of philosophy. Richness, abundance, boldness, color, but a sharp contour never, and never any *perfection*.[47]

This reciprocal friendship and esteem was lacking, however, in James's relationships with another Harvard colleague, George Santayana. Much of the latter's evaluations of James's philosophy were extremely unperceptive and often bitter; James unambiguously rejected Santayana's thought while acknowledging its originality and power. Although James rejoiced at having diverse philosophical viewpoints strongly represented on the Harvard faculty and expressed the opinion that Santayana was for that reason a valuable addition to the department, at the same time he felt that Santayana's philosophy was the "perfection of rottenness."[48] James was repelled by his "preciousness" and superciliousness; and, while Santayana *seemed* "a paragon of Emersonianism," he managed to produce a profoundly un-Emersonian philosophy: "The same things in Emerson's mouth would sound entirely different. E. receptive, expansive, as if handling life through a wide funnel with a great indraught; S. as if through a pin-point orifice that emits his cooling spray outward over the universe like a nose-disinfectant from an 'atomizer.' "[49]

Much different were James's feelings about the philosophy of Henri Bergson, which, published late in James's life, came as a strong and welcome rebuttal of the sterile abstractions of the "beast intellectualism." In Bergson's *L'Évolution Créatrice*, James saw a magisterial assertion of the central positions of Pragmatism. Ecstatically, he recommended its doctrines to F. C. S. Schiller: "It seems to me that nothing is important in comparison with that divine apparition. All *our* positions, a real time, a growing world, asserted magisterially, and the beast intellectualism killed absolutely *dead*...."[50]

Bergson's recourse to actual experiences as the authentic source for philosophical doctrines provided welcome reinforcements in the fierce battle against Intellectualist forces. In addition, James found in Bergson's work a tremendous amount of intellectual stimulation, opening up for him all sorts of new questions and bringing the old ones into "a most agreeable liquefaction."[51]

Among his most active allies and co-thinkers were an Englishman and a fellow American—F. C. S. Schiller of Oxford University and John Dewey of Chicago and Columbia. Under their respective banners—Pragmatism, Humanism, and Instrumentalism—the three fought on various fronts against a common enemy. Differing in important respects, they agreed on the need to destroy the airy abstractions of Intellectualism. Schiller and James in particular made strenuous efforts to agree with each other doctrinally in the exposition of their philosophies and in the polemics of philosophical controversies.

Schiller, who readily took to controversies, responded to attacks with an energy that discomfited James; but Schiller himself modestly considered his outbursts as moves to make room for James's advances in philosophy. In 1907, he declared to James that he and Howard Knox were guarding "your most valuable flank, and by repelling counter attacks secure your advance. Remember that just as you hear the criticism on me I hear that on you—low, petty and dishonest as it generally is. It makes me angry."[52]

Schiller proposed to James that they unite their philosophical views under a banner emblazoned *Humanism*, a label and motto well chosen, he thought, to engage the scholastic, inhuman, fossilized, and abstract forces of Intellectualism. But James, though attracted by the appeal of "Humanism," felt that his own ugly term "Pragmatism" was already too firmly established to be altered. He also believed that his views and Schiller's, though engaged in a fight for a common cause, were too different in substance to carry a common label.

James saw in Schiller's humanism a great import for life and regeneration, and he saluted "the renovating character for *all things* of Humanism. . . ." He saw both himself and Schiller as worthily engaged in exposing "the outwornness as of a scarecrow's garments, simulating life by flapping in the wind of nightfall, of all intellectualism, and the blindness and deadness of all who worship intellectualistic idols, the Royces and Taylors, and, worse than all, their followers, who, with no inward excuse of nature (being too unoriginal really to *prefer* anything) just blunder on to the wrong scent, when it is so easy to catch the right one, and then stick to it with the fidelity of inorganic matter."[53]

Apart from Schiller's unwillingness to turn the other cheek to the assaults of Intellectualists, his relatively subjectivistic theory of knowledge troubled James, who believed that Pragmatism must be based upon an objective theory of knowledge. Schiller carried the creative role of man's knowledge in the shaping of reality to a point where, James believed, being lost its objectivity. But James's faith in the essential constructiveness of Schiller's thinking was at no time ever weakened. He urged Schiller to apply himself fullheartedly to working out special problems by Humanistic methods. To the very end of his life, he cherished Schiller and his Humanism, writing three weeks before his death: "I leave the 'Cause' in your hands. . . . Good-bye and God bless you."[54]

The other ally of the "cause," John Dewey, attracted James's attention and aroused his admiration around the beginning of the twentieth century. Coming to Pragmatism from an earlier involvement with Hegel, Dewey always remained somewhat alien to James and Schiller, who traced their philosophic origins to British Empiricism. In James's *Psychology*, Dewey discovered the Instrumentalist logic which so largely shaped his own ethical theories; in 1903, he told James that the *Psychology* was the spiritual progenitor of contemporary Pragmatism, not only his but that of other thinkers. James in turn tried to learn what he could from Dewey, whose work he considered "splendid stuff." He was impressed also with the manner in which Dewey attracted young scholars to Chicago and envied that university for having a real "school" of philosophy: "A real school and real thought. At Harvard we have plenty of thought but not school."[55] "It rejoices me greatly that your School (I mean your philosophic school) at the University of Chicago is, after this long gestation, bringing its fruits to birth in a way that will demonstrate its great unity and vitality, and be a revelation to many people, of American scholarship."[56]

V Career in Psychology

James's career in psychology ties in so intimately with his subsequent absorption in philosophy that it can be viewed, among other things, as a preparation for his philosophical career. During the twelve years from 1878 to 1890 James taught psychology at Harvard and labored over the *Principles of Psychology*. To him some share of the credit must be given for creating a "new" psychology, allied with science and combining "the methods of observation with those of speculation and reflection."[57]

James's work in anatomy and physiology, along with his medical studies, made it impossible for him to be satisfied with a psychology that stressed the soul and ignored the body. His enthusiasm for evolution required that the psychological aspects of life be explained in terms compatible with the general theory of evolution. "A real science of man," he wrote in 1875, "is now being built up out of the theory of evolution and the facts of archaeology, the nervous system and the senses."[58]

He saw a vital need to shift psychology from its ethical and moral moorings and to work it into the natural sciences. He saw himself, as early as 1868, as wading his way toward psychology through the physiology of the senses;[59] and three years later he declared that the union of the two disciplines in one man was "the most natural thing in the world."[60]

> When William James proposed to make psychology a natural science, there was a rude awakening among American philosophers who, in their "critical" dogmatic slumbers, had become accustomed to the contrast between natural and moral science, as if it were the unshakable foundation of faith, as well as the customary foundation of all text books. . . . But intelligence, the life of the soul, mental activity, this field because of its teleological nature had been subordinated to moral science, *Geisteswissenschaft*, was now to be assimilated to biology. Henceforth reason was to be explained as a natural outgrowth of animal intelligence.[61]

Reason, since it is incorporated into the general life of the individual and of the human species, is not intrinsically "superior" to or transcendent to the mundane activities of life. Neither reason nor the emotions exists "for their own sake"; feeling and consciousness, like all other things, exist *because they have utility*, contributing to the well-being of the total organism.

The psychologist, James believed, must always keep the *total* interests of the concrete individual in view, seeing it as active and as occupying an environmnt. The role of the will in the intellectual life of the individual and the role of impulses and passions require attention to correct the purely intellectualistic stresses of the older Associationist psychologies. The new insights of Darwinism must be admitted to throw a "flood of light upon our instinctive and passional constitution."[62]

As a psychologist, James wished to help transform psychology into a *genuine* science. Preparatory to doing so, it was necessary to extract and remove the huge deposit of metaphysics with which psychological studies were encumbered and to articulate the questions which psychology as a natural science should properly investigate. It was necessary also to relate psychological data to the total human person, for example, relate them to physiological processes; an appropriate scientific method which would go beyond the current methods of introspection and description was required—and would be found in the psychological laboratory. Connections with biology, chemistry, and other natural sciences had to be established.

Psychology also had to be relieved of the burdens imposed upon it by those who viewed it as being a particularly "noble" discipline dealing with "seraphic insights." It had to seek the answers to practical questions, not only to enlighten students but also to relieve those who were screaming in madhouses:

> The kind of psychology which could cure a case of melancholy, or charm a chronic insane delusion away, ought cerainly to be preferred to the most seraphic insight into the nature of the soul. And that is the sort of psychology which men who care little or nothing for ultimate rationality, the biologists, nerve-doctors, and psychical researchers, namely, are surely tending, whether we help them or not, to bring about.[63]

The Man and His Career

> We need a fair and square and explicit *abandonment* of such questions as that of the soul, the transcendental ego, the fusion of ideas or particles of mind stuff, etc., by the practical man; and a fair and square determination on the part of the philosophers to keep such questions out of psychology and treat them only in their widest possible connections, among the objects of an ultimate critical review of all the elements of the world.[64]

In his efforts to make psychology a genuine natural science, rather than a "philosophy of the soul," James in 1875 developed a graduate course entitled "The Relations between Physiology and Psychology," and in 1876 he instructed undergraduates in *physiological* psychology. Apparatus for experiments was acquired, and thus there came into being, for America, about 1875, experimental psychology and the psychological laboratory.[65]

The attention devoted by James to psychological problems throughout the ensuing years up to 1890 culminated in the publication of the *Principles of Psychology*. The creative and seminal nature of this classic was extolled in 1935 by Ralph Barton Perry:

> One recent writer says that there are three schools of psychology, "the conscious, the unconscious, and the anti-conscious," referring to the introspective, the psychoanalytical, and the behavioristic schools. It is easy to find all three in James. The same may be said of the *"Gestalt"* school, or the *"Akt"* school, or the "Functional" school. James promoted the method of introspection traditional in the British school, and imported the results and techniques of the experimental school from Germany. He was interested in applied psychology and comparative psychology. His chapter [in the *Principles*] gave a great impetus to social psychology, and his medical approach and emphasis on "exceptional mental states" gave him a place in the development of abnormal psychology and psychopathology.[66]

Counterbalancing James's emphatic determination to contribute to the development of a truly *scientific* psychology were his yearnings for work in ethics, epistemology, and metaphysics.

After years of dedication to psychology, his impatience with its current state grew constantly greater. His own classical work, soon after he had written it, appeared, like most of contempory psychology, destined for the junkyard: "As 'Psychologies' go, it is a good one, but psychology is in such an ante-scientific condition that the whole present generation of them is destined to become unreadable old mediaeval lumber, as soon as the first genuine tracks of insight are made. The sooner the better, for me."[67] Psychology was waiting still for its Galileo—"not a single *elementary* law" had yet been glimpsed.[68]

In particular, James was dissatisfied because so few really creative ideas had appeared to fertilize psychology. The emphasis placed upon method and the laboratory seemed ill advised when new ideas and a better quality of thinking about psychological problems were the greater needs. So, when James finally found his way clear to move on to philosophizing professionally, he did so with a great sense of liberation, declaring, in 1896, "I feel . . . as if I had bought the right to say good-bye to psychology . . . and turn myself to more speculative directions."[69] And he wrote in 1899 that "I fear I am ceasing to be a psychologist, and becoming exclusively a moralist and metaphysician. I have surrendered all psychological teaching to Münsterberg and his assistant, and the thought of psychophysical experimentation, and altogether of brass-instrument and algebraic-formula psychology fills me with horror."[70]

James's psychological theories generally are counterparts of his views in philosophy. His "stream-of-consciousness," his "transmission" theory of the brain, his view that knowledge depends on will, and his insistence that the highest aims of psychology must be "practical," are, for example, counterparts of certain of his most fundamental views in metaphysics. His stream of thought, or stream-of-consciousness, theory, stressing the connectedness and fluidity of mental life, is the perfect psychological analogue to his Radical Empiricism, which sees reality as consisting not of isolated atoms of being but of interconnected, fluid experiences.

The theory that the brain acts not as *producer* of consciousness but as *sifter, limiter,* and *individualizer* thereof was defended, before 1897, as being psychologically tenable; in his later metaphysics and philosophy of religion James used this theory to explain mysticism and to argue for human immortality. In his "Ingersoll Lecture on the Immortality of Man," in 1898, James, in replying to the argument of "science" that the mind is dependent on the body and therefore cannot outlive it, declared that the *facts* of physiological psychology require only a "functional" dependence of mind on body. Such a dependence does not necessarily imply that the brain *produces* the mind; it may merely release it, or *let it through*. In that case the larger reservoir or "mother-sea" of consciousness would remain intact after the dissolution of the brain and might retain traces of the life history of its individual emanation.[71] Mystical experiences, in turn, occur whenever this "mother-sea" breaks through at some point of those barriers which are erected by men's individualities —the breakthrough being made possible by a shift in consciousness.

James's insistence that psychology discover a *causal* and not merely a *descriptive* account of its phenomena is a counterpart of his philosophical theory of truth. Truths must be capable of putting men into fruitful relationships with reality—a causal psychology, having discovered dynamic laws, would make possible prediction and control of human behavior. A genuinely psychophysic theory—one so much desired by clergymen, teachers, and those in charge of the mentally ill—would supersede all descriptive psychologies and make them seem insignificant.[72]

With his mind stimulated by years of dedication to psychological studies, James moved steadily into "purely" philosophical pursuits. By the end of the century, the psychologist had become the philosopher, leaving behind the study of psychology on which he had worked for years and giving way to his longings for philosophy.

CHAPTER 3

The Philosophic Enterprise: Pragmatism and Radical Empiricism

GEORGE SANTAYANA insisted that William James was not *essentially* a philosopher: "His excursions into philosophy were . . . in the nature of raids. . . ."[1] "It would be incongruous . . . to expect of him that he should build a philosophy like an edifice to go and live in for good. Philosophy to him was rather like a maze in which he happened to find himself wandering, and what he was looking for was the way out."[2] Santayana saw James as a mystic with such strong anti-intellectualistic bias that it was impossible for him to be a genuine philosopher: "He was a mystic, a mystic in love with life. He was comparable to Rousseau and Walt Whitman; he expressed a generous and tender sensibility, rebelling against sophistication, and preferring daily sights and sounds, and a vague but indomitable faith in fortune, to any settled intellectual tradition calling itself science or philosophy."[3] To Santayana, James was, therefore, hostile to genuine science—despite his degree in medicine, his teaching of physiology, and his contributions to psychology!

I *Angle of Vision*

William James became a philosopher to satisfy a profound need which penetrated every aspect of his being. His health—physical, emotional, and mental—was contingent upon his finding the answers to philosophic problems—no mere riddles for him but indispensable keys to being. These problems brought him, before he found satisfactory answers, to despair and to the brink of self-destruction. When the answers were formulated, they retained, because of the intention of the philosopher, the signature of their origins. James considered the philosophy and the philosopher inseparably linked, like the artist and his work. Even the most general of statements, having a personal origin,

Pragmatism and Radical Empiricism

he saw as bearing with it a personal note. The *human* origins of philosophy James accepts and honors; the authentic *personal* elements are retained and utilized. Every genuine problem is seen as *someone's* problem; every truth is *some thinker's* truth. The individual and universal human features in philosophical thinking are not to be exorcized; they are to be purified, accepted on their merits, and given central roles in the creation of the philosopher's picture of reality.

The first philosophical problem which concerned James in a deeply personal way was that of free will, or, as he called it, "determinism versus indeterminism." Given the best scientific viewpoints of his day, the individual seemed to be compelled to believe that man is completely determined in all his actions, physical, mental, and moral. James, familiar with the science of his day, felt compelled to see himself and others as mere automata, manipulated by forces beyond their control. This belief satisfied those requirements of his being which called for scientific consistency, but it violated other beliefs and yearnings of which he was painfully conscious. These too demanded recognition and satisfaction, for example, the consciousness of moral responsibility, which required some areas of human freedom to have meaning and fulfillment.

James's early expressions on the subject of determinism revealed his mixed feelings—a reverence for science, which seemed to require determinism, and an equally strong respect for the ethical element in life, which required moral autonomy. "I feel," he wrote, "we are Nature through and through, that we are wholly conditioned, that not a wiggle of ours will happen save as the result of physical laws; and yet, notwithstanding, we are *en rapport* with reason. How to conceive it? Who knows?"[4]

The only intellectually respectable solution to the problem evident to James at the time was determinism, with its attendant sacrifice of all the moral significance in human lives. James's early acceptance of determinism involved despair and agony; and he clung to the hope that he would find an intellectually honest way to affirm freedom. When he was twenty-five, he thus recorded his feelings: "I find myself more and more drifting towards sensationalism closed in by scepticism—but the scepticism will keep bursting out in the very midst of it, too, from time to time; so that I cannot help thinking I may one day get a glimpse of things through the ontological window. At present it is walled up."⁵

When James took up his vocation as a philosopher, he found himself approaching the great, perennial problems with the hope of vindicating man's volitional nature against the "intellectual" arguments which regarded free will as a mere fiction. When he examined, for example, the basic metaphysical nature of human beings, he took into account not only the demands and aspirations of man's intellect but also the demands and aspirations of his volitional and emotional nature. As he developed his philosophy, it became clearly an attempt to see reality in terms of all the resources of the human person, taking into account not only his passive speculator role in the world but also his creator role in engendering new realities and introducing new relationships and organizations into the existing order.

In James's philosophy, man is frankly and unapologetically taken as a major key to the nature of reality—not just man viewed as knowing but as doing, not just man viewed as intellect but as an emotional, volitional, creative being. James insists that man is *present* in the reality which philosophy investigates; he argues that the objective study of reality must include, not expunge, man with his various so-called subjective elements. Man's desires are seen as being as much a part of reality as the tides and rainfall; they are not to be dismissed merely because of intellectualistic biases against them. Out of a patient, profound study of the *world*, in which man plays a part, and of *man*, in which the world plays a part, there could emerge a philosophy as close to truth as man can hope to come.

II *The Nature of Philosophy*

Emerson defined the scholar as *man thinking*; William James said, "Philosophy in the full sense is only *man thinking*, thinking about generalities rather than about particulars."⁶ Both sage and philosopher agreed that there is no thinking apart from the *thinking individual*; scholarship and philosophy, no matter how removed in presentation from their personal origins, are human products. Behind the volume and in it is a writer, with all his fallibility and aspirations as man and as thinker.

One of the most dangerous pitfalls of philosophizing, James

saw, is the tendency to think of philosophy as an objective, independent entity, existing apart from human beings and enjoying an enviable sort of superiority. The tendency to think in such a manner is reenforced by traditions which regard the human intellect, at its best, as participating in an eternal, ideal order of being. But, actually, philosophy is, inevitably, one other human production, bearing the undeniable marks of human limitations. No matter how greatly various human enterprises may differ, from the noblest achievements to the most wretched failures, they all bear the benchmarks of a very imperfect race of artisans.

This human imperfection is visible in every philosophy and cannot be entirely overcome—because man's means of philosophic understanding and expression are forever inadequate in dealing with the richnesses of reality. Insofar as philosophy means the articulate and the scientifically accurate, it will not be able perfectly to formulate reality. "Life and mysticism," as James observed, "exceed the articulate."[7] This incomplete adequation between philosophy and reality is partly due to the fact that reason does not encompass all of reality, and can handle only parts of it. Other parts can be handled only by emotions or mystical intuition—and must be left to unphilosophical activities.

The limitations which reason suffers from, as it encounters reality, are described in an unpublished note which James wrote in 1905: "Reason doesn't surround Being. It encounters it. Feeling only, life, penetrates being. Reason is secondary. Illustrate by water and marble, or lime which it [water] only partially dissolves. Always refractory remainder, 'surd,' brute fact. A very natural state of things, if we agree that the intellect is a supervening faculty, added for its utility in handling what it finds, but not coeval with creation."[8]

Reason can operate most effectively and make its best contributions to life and to philosophy when its limitations and legitimate goals are understood. Reason must not operate in a fashion that violates the character of reality or denies the legitimate roles of emotions and will. Reason has indeed so operated in those philosophies which aim at establishing "schematisms with permanent and absolute distinctions": "All neat schematicisms with permanent and absolute distinctions, classifications with absolute pretensions, systems with pigeon holes, etc., have

[47]

this character [of the artificial]. All 'classic,' clean, cut and dried, 'noble,' 'fixed,' 'eternal.' Weltanshauungen seemed to me to violate the character with which life concretely comes and the expression which it bears, of being, or at least involving, a muddle and a struggle, with an 'ever not quite' to all our formulas, and novelty and possibility forever leaking in."[9]

If permanent and absolute distinctions, absolute classifications, and static systems are supposed to be avoided, can there indeed be such a thing as philosophy? Emphatically *yes*, says James—and philosophy in all its branches, including metaphysics, ethics, and epistemology. Philosophy may well be among man's greatest achievements, and, properly constructed, one of his most practical creations in the conduct of life. Metaphysics in particular may be regarded as the "most exquisite work of human mind," although its progress to the present time is indeed "pathetic."[10]

Nevertheless, it must be pointed out that there are approaches to philosophic problems which lead inevitably to conclusions that are arid, pedantic, and petty. Taking such approaches is a worse course than having no articulate philosophy at all. And developing a philosophy which does no more than confirm "common sense" seems to be a process hardly worth the trouble.

> Of all forms of earthly worry, the metaphysical worry seems most gratuitous. If it lands us in permanently skeptical conclusions, it is worse than superfluous; and if (as is almost always the case with non-skeptical systems) it simply ends by "indorsing" common-sense, and reinstating us in the possession of our old feelings, motives, and duties, we may fairly ask if it was worth while to go so far round in order simply to return to our starting-point . . . Is not the primal state of philosophic innocence, since the practical difference is *nil*, as good as the state of reflective enlightenment?[11]

Philosophy, to produce good results, must be approached with freshness of outlook; while the philosophical achievements of the past should not be ignored, neither should they lead one to give up all attempts at original thinking in one's own day. Instead of being overawed by existing official answers or technical apparatus, one should remember that one's experiences are the greatest of source books. Each generation ought to attack things "as if there were no official answer preoccupying the field." But, unfortunately, as James observed, "We work with one eye on the problem, and with the other on the consequences to our enemy or to our lawgiver, as the case may be; the result in both cases is mediocrity."[12]

Technicality and remoteness from the inspiration of living experiences both spell failure in philosophy: "In a subject like philosophy it is really fatal to lose connexion with the open air of human nature, and to think in terms of shop-tradition only."[13] Closeness to the concrete details of life is not an evil to be overcome but an ideal to be pursued: "In the end philosophers may get into as close contact as realistic novelists with the facts of life."[14] This closeness to the concrete facts of life is incompatible with excessive technicalities; as James's admirer Howard Knox observed, "James seems always to have felt that such philosophic truths as were intrinsically incapable of conveyance in nontechnical form must also be intrinsically of but slight importance for human guidance."[15]

The aim of the philosopher is not to construct—or discover— some changeless order of ideal beings and then formulate a description of it in rigid, technical terms. To do so would violate the nature of being, which constantly reveals itself as restless and fluid, perpetually growing and changing. The aim of the philosopher must rather be *to find paths* in this constantly expanding and pulsating universe:

> Philosophers are after all like poets. They are pathfinders. What every one can feel, what every one can know in the bone and marrow of him, they sometimes can find words for and express! The words and thoughts of the philosophers are not exactly the words and thoughts of the poets—worse luck. But both alike have the same function. They are, if I may use a simile, so many spots, or blazes,—blazes made by the axe of the human intellect on the trees of the otherwise trackless forests of human experience. They give you somewhere to go from. They give you a direction and a place to reach. They do not give you the integral forest with all its sunlit glories and its moonlit witcheries and wonders.[16]

This philosopher-pathfinder will never write a complete, definitive geography of "the woods" because they are forever expanding beyond the scope of his equipment and efforts. His descriptions and maps will never encompass all the woods, but he will explore as many areas as he can, and mark off trails where others may follow and, if they wish, open up new trails of their own.

The great achievement of philosophy down to the present time has *not* been, therefore, its answers to specific problems, which are forever being challenged, but rather the deepening of consciousness in the human race and the opening up of new areas of awareness. In this achievement the work of the philosophers has shown a genuine superiority over the works of men of narrower and more "practical" interests:

> For as yet philosophy has celebrated hardly any stable achievements. The labors of philosophers have, however, been confined to deepening enormously the philosophic *consciousness*, and revealing more and more minutely and fully the import of metaphysical problems. In this preliminary task ontologists and phenomenologists, mechanists and teleologists must join friendly hands, for each has been indispensable to the work of the other, and the only foe of either is the common foe of both—namely, the practical, conventionally thinking man, to whom . . . nothing has true seriousness but personal interests . . . [17]

Individual philosophers, constantly examining, enlarging, and clarifying the philosophic positions which appeal to them, contribute to mankind's expanding awareness of reality. For the student who undertakes to study this philosophical accumulation, there is offered the possibility of finding illuminating, though not final, answers to the classic questions of life. But there is also another equally, if not more, important reward: the reorganization of his own ways of thinking along lines of genuine philosophical wisdom. Such ways of thinking will enable him to escape from inferior modes of thought enfeebled by convention, common sense, and tradition: "philosophic study," he will find, "means the habit of always seeking an alternative, of not taking the usual for granted, of making conventionalities fluid again, of imagining foreign states of mind. In a word it means the possession of mental perspective."[18]

Thus, the student of philosophy is rewarded not only with the answers and meditations of great men—he is also repaid for his efforts by a most desirable sort of self-transformation. In this very transformation he will find the chief *educational* value of philosophic studies, a transformation which penetrates *every* area of the student's mental activities: "As for philosophy, technically so called, or the reflection of man on his relations with the universe, its educational essence lies in the quickening of the spirit to its *problems*. What doctrines students take from their teachers are of little consequence provided they catch from them the living, philosophic attitude of mind, the independent, personal look at all the data of life, and the eagerness to harmonize them."[19]

Catching the spirit of the problems of philosophy involves the student not only in alterations, for the better, in his intellectual life but also brings his intellect, will, taste, and emotions to new awarenesses and new relationships. In responding to the challenges of philosophic problems, the student responds with his entire person; and in organizing his answers to the problems, he is rewarded with an awakening and a reorganization of his own self. In this process the role of the intellect is indispensable but definitely not exclusive: "The whole man within us is at work when we form our philosophic opinions. Intellect, will, taste, and passion co-operate just as they do in practical affairs."[20]

Although philosophy has made certainly as much progress as any human discipline in history, it has not yet produced answers which satisfy the bona fide inquirer. The would-be philosopher must acknowledge this fact and try to profit by the lessons of the past:

> By what title is it that every would-be universal formula, every system of philosophy, which rears its head, receives the inevitable critical volley from one half of mankind, and falls to the rear, to become at the very best the creed of some partial sect? Either it has dropped out of its net some of our impressions of sense,— what we call the facts of nature,—or it has left the theoretic and defining department with a lot of inconsistencies and unmediated transitions on its hands; or else, finally, it has left some one or more of our fundamental active and emotional powers with no object outside of themselves to react on or to live for. Any one of these defects is fatal to its complete success.[21]

James hopes to avoid these defects by linking philosophy to the whole man and by avoiding the unrealistic procedure of erecting philosophy upon abstractions which themselves deny all those parts of reality which lie outside the abstractions. For this aim he was to be called a non-philosopher by some; by others, he was declared to be a great liberator of the human spirit.

III A Reformed Philosophy

The philosophy of William James is not indeed a mansion among the great mansions of philosophy; it does not have the classical outlines of Aristotle's system, which explains the movements of the heavenly bodies and incorporates the Unmoved Mover in a universe explainable by universal formulas. James's philosophy is a humbler thing—a guide to the human traveler in this world.

The questions and answers of James's philosophy emerge from certain vital, central insights—much as the pattern of a bird's or animal's life develops in response to its goals and environment. These philosophic insights of James are humanistic; they are anthropocentric—the human person is placed at the center of his philosophy (subject, later, to the central position of the role of God). From man's total personality emerges a philosophy which is humanistic, pragmatic, and experiential, vindicating man's faith in his highest ideals and encouraging his noblest efforts for the well-being of himself and his fellow men.

An examination of the philosophic heritage of the West discloses a vast quantity of deadwood which each generation hauls through life. Much of this deadwood has come to occupy positions in various philosophies, and it kills much that is vital in life and thought. The anti-humanistic traditions of philosophy deserve not veneration but expulsion from the realms of philosophic activity. To free men from these hereditary idols of philosophy, William James fashioned a number of highly effective instruments; and among the most successful are Pragmatism and Radical Empiricism Pragmatism and Radical Empiricism are pivotal theories in this philosophy; they are also, unfortunately, among the most misunderstood and misrepresented teachings in modern philosophy, particularly the doctrine of Pragmatism. Radical Empiricism and Pragmatism, once properly appreciated, offer the best angles from which to view the philosophy of William James.

IV Pragmatism

The commonest simplification holds that Pragmatism judges a belief by its *practical* consequences: by determining whether it produces results which are *useful* or *not useful*. This description, though apparently supported by occasional inexact utterances of William James, invites misunderstanding and should be rejected in favor of another deceptively simple but more precise statement. More exactly, Pragmatism means that concepts should be reduced to their *positive experienceable operations*.[22]

In the theory of Pragmatism, James appeals to philosophers to examine their reasons for being interested in philosophy in the first place. He asks them, in effect, to put aside their philosophical biases and find for themselves the authentic reasons—apart from snobbery—for philosophical enterprise and their participation in it. In seeking such information, the philosopher will find it more fruitful to transpose the general question about philosophy into some specific counterparts. Instead of asking, "Why study philosophy?," he should inquire why he should investigate specific problems of philosophy, such as God, free will, immortality. If these problems and their answers cannot be reduced to positive experienceable operations in human life, then the philosopher must conclude that such problems are lacking in that seriousness which is essential to genuine knowledge. On the other hand, if specific concepts are found to have positive experienceable operations in life, the pragmatic insight can then be used further to explore their meanings.

Pragmatism—at once a method, a "genetic theory of what is meant by truth,"[23] "*a general theory of human action*,"[24] and a program for philosophy—is pregnant with unforeseen depths and possibilities. James confessed his own difficulties in coming to a fuller awareness of the meanings of Pragmatism. Bergson, writing to James, declared, "I ceaselessly repeat . . . that pragmatism is one of the most subtle and *nuancées* doctrines that have ever appeared in philosophy (just because this doctrine reinstates truth in the flux of experience), and one is sure to go wrong if one speaks of pragmatism before reading you *as a whole*."[25] As late as 1906, James himself referred to the difficulties in attaining knowledge of Pragmatism: "I myself have been slow in coming into the full inwardness of pragmatism. Schiller's writings and those of Dewey and his school have taught me some of its wider reaches."[26]

The principle of Pragmatism, first of all, aids in determining which concepts are worthy of investigation and then provides the criterion for judging their value. Concepts which *cannot* be reduced to positive experienceable operations do not warrant study by the philosopher. Among such concepts are the so-called metaphysical attributes of God as distinguished from His moral attributes—such metaphysical attributes as His indivisibility, His repudiation of inclusion in a genus, and His aseity. Even though one were forced by "a coercive logic" to believe these metaphysical attributes, one would be free to ask "how do such qualities make any definite connection with our life? And if they severally call for no distinctive adaptations of our conduct, what vital difference can it possibly make to a man's religion whether they be true or false?"[27]

On the other hand, the concepts associated with God's *moral* attributes *do* make a difference in a man's life and possess, therefore, positive experienceable operations for the believer: "Pragmatically, they stand on an entirely different footing. They determine fear and hope and expectation, and are foundations for the saintly life."[28] Pragmatically, the concept of God's holiness, for example, is significant because it means, in terms of man's positive experienceable operations, that being holy, God can will nothing but the good. Likewise, His omnipotence signifies that He can secure the triumph of the good: "Being omniscient, he can see us in the dark. Being just, he can punish us for what he sees. Being loving, he can pardon too. Being unalterable, we can count on him securely. These qualities enter into connection with our life, it is highly important that we should be informed concerning them."[29]

For first enunciating the principle of Pragmatism James acknowledged a debt to Charles Sanders Peirce and frequently called attention to Peirce's historic article "How to Make our Ideas Clear," published in 1878.[30] In 1902 James summarized the contents of Peirce's article, accepting it without criticism:

> Thought in movement has for its only conceivable motive the attainment of belief, or thought at rest. Only when our thought about a subject has found its rest in belief can our action on the subject firmly and safely begin. Beliefs, in short, are rules for action; and the whole function of thinking is but one step in the production of active habits. If there were any part of a thought that made no difference in the thought's practical consequences, then that part would be no proper element of the thought's significance. To develop a thought's meaning we need therefore

only determine what conduct it is fitted to produce; that conduct is for us its sole significance; and the tangible fact at the root of all our thought-distinctions is that there is no one of them so fine as to consist in anything but a difference of practice. To attain perfect clearness in our thoughts of an object, we need then only consider what sensations, immediate or remote, we are conceivably to expect from it, and what conduct we must prepare in case the object be true. Our conception of these practical consequences is for us the whole of our conception of the object, so far as that conception has positive significance at all. This is the principle of Peirce, the principle of pragmatism.[31]

This principle of Pragmatism is a clue or compass, "by following which," said James, "I find myself more and more confirmed in believing that we may keep our feet upon the proper trail."[32] The needle of that compass points to the positive experienceable operations connected with concepts; it does so not only for relatively unimportant concepts but also for the largest and most important concepts in human knowledge: ". . . the whole function of philosophy ought to be to find out what definite difference it will make to you and to me, at definite instants of our life, if this world-formula or that world-formula be the one which is true."[33]

In 1907, three years before his death, James reported that he had grown "more and more deeply into pragmatism" and declared that it was "absolutely the only philosophy with *no* humbug." At the same time, he expressed a hope that his readers would be careful to distinguish in his own philosophy between Pragmatism and Radical Empiricism, which have "no necessary connexion with each other."[34]

V Radical Empiricism

"I give the name of 'radical empiricism' to my *Weltanschauung*,"[35] declared James. "My philosophy is what I call a radical empiricism, a pluralism, which represents order as being gradually won and always in the making."[36] James, who admired his empirical predecessors in Britain, John Locke, George Berkeley, and David Hume, believed that the empirical British spirit in philosophy was intellectually, practically, and morally on the sane, sound, and true path.[37] But, at the same time, James was far from complete accord with the "classical" or "pure" empiricism of the British school; among other things, he criticized British empiricism for being *insufficiently* empirical, especially in Hume's failure to recognize *experienced conjunctive relations.* Therefore, he thought it necessary to give his own variety of empiricism a distinctive name, and chose to call it *Radical* Empiricism to emphasize its profoundly empiricist nature: its total marriage to experience in all its aspects.

James's education had given him an ideal preparation for being the founder of Radical Empiricism and had equipped him for the arduous task of treating experience with respect and understanding. Thanks to education and temperament, he was able to be a consistent empiricist. One observer reported: "His materials are facts. He deals with actual experience. To this he came not only by the natural disposition of his mind, but by the processes of his education. His first degree was not in arts but in medicine. He was studying bodies when his contemporaries were studying books."[38]

In equating reality with experience, James, contrary to possible expectations, does not constrict the boundaries of reality. By including *all* experiences within reality, he avoids reducing reality to certain particular types of experiences. He includes experiences of the vague and incoherent as well as the clear and distinct; so called appearances as well as so-called realities; the subjective as well as the objective; the emotional as well as the intellectual; the unorthodox, the mystical, the non-respectable are all included from the outset. No experience, regardless of its source, is excluded *a priori*; all are admitted provisionally, subject later to the closest study on the basis of their performances and interdigitation with the rest of experience.

In his attempts to understand the general outlines of reality, the Radical Empiricist deliberately excludes the hedges and walls introduced by materialists and idealists, Platonists and Cartesians, and other earlier philosophers. In his preparation to study being, the Radical Empiricist endeavors to purify his mind of the theories of philosophy so that he can *take the fundamental aspects of consciousness at their face value*, receiving them and examining them patiently without rushing them into categories and classifications, without judging them hastily in *a priori* terms.

Bent on the study of experience, the Radical Empiricist is

like a naturalist studying a living wild animal in its native habitat—as opposed to a museum specialist interested only in assigning a dead specimen to its proper place in his chart of the animal kingdom. The so-called "superiority" of the techniques of the museum specialist is "proved" by the neatness and clearness of his conclusions, which, however, are obtainable only by ignoring most of the realities of the non-museum parts of the world.

All experiences, all data of consciousness, are in some way real; and none of them should be denied to be real simply because they cannot be fitted into the museums which men have constructed. Every datum is an epiphany of reality. No matter how humble it may appear to be, a full appreciation of its meaning might reveal consequences of revolutionary dimensions. *Every fact,* said Emerson, *is an epiphany of God!*

"What is it to be 'real'?" inquired James. "The best definition I know," he replied, "is that which the pragmatist rule gives: 'anything is real of which we find ourselves obliged to take account in any way.' Concepts are thus as real as percepts, for we cannot live a moment without taking account of them."[39] And, likewise, faith is real, moral responsibility is real, and the ideals by which men live are real, no matter how poorly they may have been formulated by philosophers.

While Radical Empiricism affirms the reality of all experiences, it also denies, with equal emphasis, the unreality of all things that have been alleged to exist beyond experience. The Unknown of Herbert Spencer, the thing-in-itself of Kant, and the world of ideas of Plato, being extra-experiential, are therefore denied to exist. All such alleged beings, invented to explain and make more intelligible the objects which men experience, are rejected by the Radical Empiricist for the reason that *beings* which men experience cannot be made more intelligible by reference to "beings" which lie, by their very nature, beyond man's experience. Those who fear and distrust human experience look for security in transempirical "realities," assuming that experience is unintelligible; and, in so doing, they make *the* greatest error of philosophy.

If the data of experience are to be regarded as intelligible and if some of our beliefs about these data are to be verified, such intelligibility and verification must be sought within the context of experience itself. Philosophers must resist the very natural tendency to think in *dualistic* analogies about reality. They must not think of experience in terms of an ambassador who can be recognized only by the credentials which he bears from another, and superior, person. This analogy will not work if it is carried to the very frontiers of metaphysics—there are no grounds for assuming a reality beyond experience and, more significantly, no practical reason for wishing to make such an assumption.

Philosophers need not assume or "prove" a being beyond experience because, as study will show, experience itself bears its own credentials and carries its own inner intelligibility. This intelligibility is to be found potentially in the data of concrete moments of consciousness and in the relationships of such data. Potential intelligibility is present in experience, and man is capable of organizing experience in a rational manner. This fact is extolled by Walt Whitman:

> Mine is no callous shell,
> I have instant conductors all over me whether I pass, or stop,
> They seize every object and lead it harmless through me.
> . . . .
> All truths wait in all things,
> They neither hasten their own delivery nor resist it,
> They do not need the obstetric forceps of the surgeon,
> The insignificant is as big to me as any,
> (What is less or more than a touch.)
> . . . .
> I know I am solid and sound
> To me the converging objects of the universe perpetually flow,
> All are written to me, and I must get what the writing means.[40]

This respect for experience, this listening to the message of the present moment, is the fulcrum on which James shifts philosophy to a new orientation. This orientation brings radical changes in the understanding of change, time, unity, plurality, the subjective, the objective—all of the categories, in fact, of philosophical thinking. All of reality will be conceived no longer in the light of old analogies but now in the analogy of *moments of experience*: "If empiricism is to be radical it must indeed admit the concrete data of experience in their full completeness. The only fully complete concrete data are, however, the successive moments of our own several histories, taken with their subjective personal aspect, as well as with their 'objective' deliverance or 'content.' *After the analogy of these moments of experience must all complete reality be conceived.*"⁴¹

Philosophical deliverance from ignorance about being is achieved in *understanding concrete moments of experience*. The answers to the major questions of philosophy are to be organized out of these moments of experience. What God and man are shall be understood by studying the flower in the crannied wall!

Full faithfulness to the concrete moments of experience carries Radical Empiricism into a fuller knowledge of reality, one far richer than that afforded by the older, British empiricism. Hume's Empiricism, for example, was inadequate because it introduced *a priori* distinctions into judgments about experience. These distinctions led Hume to deny the concrete existence of conjunctive relations, which the Radical Empiricist declares *can be found* in concrete experience. Hume was hampered by his *incompletely* empirical approach, and his philosophy was accordingly impoverished. James wrote: "Every examiner of the sensible life *in concreto* must see that relations of every sort, of time, space, difference, likeness, change, rate, cause, or what not, are just as integral members of the sensational flux as terms are, and that conjunctive relations are just as true members of the flux as disjunctive relations are. This is what . . . I have called the 'radically empiricist' doctrine. . . ."⁴²

While the Radical Empiricist emphasizes the fact that the sensible life is extremely rich, he does not mean to imply that reality is revealed only in the most naïve and unsophisticated experiences. Starting with the data of consciousness, the Radical Empiricist embarks upon a study of experience, which reveals a variety of types, all calling for the most exacting and creative thinking and observation.

This deep study of experience led James to enlarge the meaning of *experience* when he was writing *The Principles of Psychology*. In the last chapter of that book, as he discussed *necessary truths*, he found it necessary to "try to ascertain just how far the connections of things in the outward environment can account for our tendency to think of, and to react upon, certain things in certain ways and in no other, even though personally we have had of the things in question no experience, or almost no experience, at all."⁴³ (In the *Psychology* James provisionally assumed the common-sense dualistic distinction between knower and objects known, a distinction which is radically foreign to his philosophy.) In this chapter, written about 1885, James indicated that "the choice will then remain to us either of denying the experiential origin of certain of our judgments, or of enlarging the meaning of the word experience. . . ."[44] Since there was no intention of denying the experiential origin of any valid belief, it was necessary to enlarge the meaning of the term *experience*.

Experience in the limited, and usual, sense of that word means the experience of something foreign that is supposed to impress us. The mind's habits copy the habits of impressions, so that "our images of things assume a time- and space-arrangement which resembles the time- and space-arrangements outside."[45] (This dualistic mode of expression is not to be understood literally.) "*'The order of experience'* in this matter of the time- and space-conjunction of things is thus an indisputably *vera causa* of our forms of thought. . . . If *all* the connections among ideas in the mind could be interpreted as so many combinations of sense-data wrought into fixity in this way from without, then experience in the common sense of that word would be the sole fashioner of the mind."[46]

But much of mental life cannot be referred to such an origin. Man's "higher aesthetic, moral, and intellectual life" seems to require a different genesis, and this can be found by considering the two modes of operating which are found in "nature." In the physiological realm, for example, "nature" may make a man's ears ring

> by the sound of a bell, or by a dose of quinine; make us see yellow by spreading a field of buttercups before our eye, or by mixing a little santomine powder with our food. . . . *In the one case the natural agents produce perceptions which take cognizance of the agents themselves; in the other, they produce perceptions which take cognizance of something else.* What is taught to the mind by the "experience" in the first case, is the *order of the experience itself*. . . . But in the case of the *other* sort of natural agency, what is taught to the mind has nothing to do with the agency itself, but with some different outer relation altogether.[47]

Following out the implications of Radical Empiricism, James came to formulate them in terms of "pure experience." Despite all the profound difficulties involved in the hypothesis of pure experience, he was convinced that that hypothesis would solve the most important problems in philosophy. The "experience philosophy" offers solutions to the great problems created by the dualistic hypothesis, for example, without plunging into the unacceptable hypothesis of monism. Dualism—with its realms of matter and spirit, its distinctions between the knower and the known—makes for ease of expression and respects the individuality of beings. But it creates an unbridgeable chasm between parts of reality. Monism, on the other hand, provides unity but does so at the expense of individuality and personal freedom. Radical Empiricism, unimpeded by the abstractions of monism or dualism, seeks the truth in experience itself.

Experience has several aspects. The first, called "pure," is that aspect wherein man has not yet introduced distinctions, made selections, or established any kind of order. Associations and relationships have not yet been established as patterns for viewing experiences. No order, practical or theoretical, has yet been extracted or imposed. This "pure experience" is intrinsically neither objective nor subjective. "What we experience, what *comes before us*, is a chaos of fragmentary impressions interrupting each other . . ."[48] " 'Pure experience' is . . . the immediate flux of life which furnishes the material to our later reflection with its conceptual categories. Only new-born babes or men in a semi-coma . . . may be assumed to have an experience pure in the literal sense of a *that* which is not yet any definite *what*, tho' ready to be all sorts of whats. . . ."[49]

At the outset, the *purity* of pure experience reveals none of those distinctions which come as a result of conceptualizing. In it are to be found both the unity and the diversity needed for the solution of philosophy's most important problems. Its priority to distinctions discloses the fundamental unity of subject and object, knower and known; the discreteness revealed in data provide the basis for individuality and pluralism.

One of the tasks of philosophy is to *reconstruct* pure experience *before* it has been conceptualized and to describe reality in the terms thus gained.[50] The conceptualization of pure experience must be scrutinized to see wherein the order of nature is violated by imposing upon it patterns which are alien to its nature. Patterns are indeed necessary for men to put pure experience into forms in which it can be handled successfully; but some patterns, now firmly established, violate the nature of experience. The philosopher's task is to identify such mis-formations of reality (for example, the distortions of "vicious intellectualism"): "Make clear my own position between *pure* empiricism (tabula rasa, with impressions adding themselves . . . and no connate mental structure at all) and Kant's. There is mental structure, but the congruence of nature with it is a painfully attained compromise in which much mental structure has to be thrown away. The most *essential* features of our mental structure, viz. grammar and logic, *violate* the order of nature, as on reflexion we believe it to exist."[51]

As experience gives men new materials to digest, these materials are assimilated, rejected, or rearranged in terms of the masses of beliefs which they already possess. Most of these beliefs, or "apperceiving ideas," are common-sense traditions of the race which once were genuine discoveries of some individuals, like the comparatively modern discoveries of energy or reflex action. In their attempts "to get the chaos of their crude individual experiences into a more shareable and manageable shape," early men formulated the notions of one time and one space as single continuous receptacles, distinguished between thoughts and things, between permanent objects and changing attributes. These and other conquests, made in the distant past, are now "part of the very structure of our mind."

As a matter of fact, *some* of these ancestral discoveries are so deeply entrenched in the human mind that no experience could upset them. The concept of one time and one space and the concept of permanently existing things are so useful that men are obliged to stand by them. These beliefs "apperceive every experience and assign it to its place."[52] Their validity is attested to by their usefulness to men in organizing their lives. If these beliefs should, however, by failing to collaborate with other useful beliefs, prove to be useless, they ought to be discarded, no matter how well they may be entrenched in man's world picture.

Transformed extensively as it is, pure experience is nevertheless not an unknowable or a mysterious thing-in-itself. Like the primitive earth in the cultivated fields, it is always present and

Pragmatism and Radical Empiricism

constantly transformed. It is not behind, or below, or outside man's experience; it is the very stuff of subjective experience. The dance and the dancer are one, said Emerson; pure experience is identical with the so-called natures of the *"things"* experienced. There is no *general* stuff of which experience at large is made. "If you ask what any one bit of pure experience is made of, the answer is always the same: 'It is made of *that*, of just what appears, of space, of intensity, of flatness, brownness, or what not. . . . Experience is only a collective name for these sensible natures, and save for time and space (and, if you like, for 'being') there appears no universal element of which all things are made."[53]

The dance and the dancer are one indeed. *Thought* and *thing* refer to the same reality, and differ from one another only functionally: *"Thoughts in the concrete are made of the same stuff as things are."*[54] "There *is* no stuff anywhere but data. Within data are two parts, the objective and the subjective parts, *seen retrospectively*. . . ."[55] Moreover, James says

> The first great pitfall from which such radical standing by of experience will save us is an artificial conception of the *relations between knower and known*. Throughout the history of philosophy the subject and its object have been treated as absolutely discontinuous entities. . . . All the while, in the very bosom of the finite experience, every conjunction required to make the relation intelligible is given in full.[56]
>
> . . . .
>
> . . . the paper seen and the seeing of it are only two names for one indivisible fact which, properly named, is *the datum, the phenomenon, or the experience*. The paper is in the mind and the mind is around the paper, because paper and mind are only two names that are given later to the one experience, when, taken in a larger world of which it forms a part, its connections are traced in different directions. *To know immediately, then, or intuitively, is for mental content and object to be identical.* This is a very different definition from that which we gave of representative knowledge; but neither definition involves those mysterious notions of self-transcendency and presence in absence which are such essential parts of the ideas of knowledge, both of philosophers and of common men.[57]

Some indication of the nature of pure experience can be distilled from the fleeting moment in which one confronts a datum before proceeding to conceptualize it. Such a moment may occur when the inattentive driver notes the traffic light flick from red to green without grasping immediately the significance of the change. He stares at the light, observes its color, but fails momentarily to classify it in the category of signals. When he finally realizes that there is a signal function in the light, he has moved from a fairly "pure experience" of the colored light to a conceptualized, social reconstruction of the datum. He has made in a fraction of a second an observation, selection, rejection, and synthesis. He has transformed a datum which had no functional value into a conceptualized experience.

This conceptualizing means selecting from the vast jungle of pure experience those data which can be made useful to men and rejecting those of no value. It means also sorting data into categories: subjective and objective, the knower and those which are known. Conceptualizing may lead to errors, for example, by postulating entities such as consciousness, the soul, or substance; and, in so doing, it violates the data of pure experience.

The differences between pure experience and the reconstructed experience by which men live are great, but they are not radically disjoined. Except in the instances in which men have substituted a fiction for fact, as when they affirm that consciousness is an entity, the parts of reconstructed experience can be referred to data of pure experience as their origin.

The conceptualizing of pure experience—the using of ideas to select and organize data—is legitimate as a general process because *concepts (as well as percepts) are given in experience*: "If we take conceptual manifolds, or memories, or fancies, they also are in their first intention mere bits of pure experience, and, as such, are single *thats* which act in one context as objects, and in another context figure as mental states."[58] These non-perceptual experiences have objectivity as well as subjectivity; they are every bit as real as percepts are. Both can determine present conduct, and both are parts of reality of which men must take account. Both come at first as a chaos of experience, in which lines of order are soon traced. This tracing of lines of order introduces the problem of human knowledge; epistemology now occupies the attention of the philosopher.

CHAPTER 4

Human Knowledge

THE BELIEF that Pragmatism must be a "simple" doctrine is indeed false, and its subtlety and depth are especially evident when one examines James's theory of knowledge. But, as Bergson observed, people picture Pragmatism as something that must necessarily be simple, as "something that it should be possible to sum up in a formula."[1] In writing of James's theory of knowledge, for example, Bergson referred to the great difficulty people would have in understanding how the pragmatist, with his distinction between truth and reality, could be a realist. This difficulty, he said, came from habits of mind and habits of speech which were both formed in the Platonic mould. Man's habits of mind and speech *lead him to identify reality and truth* —contrary to James's revolutionary disjunction of the two.[2]

On this subject James was persistently misunderstood, much to his own annoyance and to the puzzlement and irritation of his critics. They criticized his disjoining of truth and reality, condemned him for alleged subjectivism, and completely misunderstood his doctrine that a belief is true if it "works." As late as 1907, only three years before his death, James was still complaining about the persistent failure of his critics to understand what he was saying; and he declared that this misunderstanding was breeding in him "a sort of despair as to whether there's any use in discussion. . . ."[3]

The widespread, persistent inability of intelligent men to understand James's meanings can be explained only in terms of the fundamental differences in speech and thought (as Bergson declared) which separate James from his critics. Both parties are using language and ways of thinking which were developed specifically to express a world view which James rejected and

[65]

which his critics continued to accept. For example, almost every phrase one can think of suggests that one is dealing with "fixed concepts and referring to some systematic scheme of thought," but James was trying to express the contrary: *"we are introducing a fluid method of dealing with an experience which itself is in a state of endless flux."*[4] This problem is clearly explained by L. P. Jacks:

> It is the habit of our minds to regard every term as containing a fixed and definite meaning, every proposition as holding within its four corners exactly what we want to convey, no more and no less. We define our terms in advance and then apply them to their uses. But the pragmatist when speaking of concrete experience employs language in quite another way. Its meanings lie not within but beyond itself; they arise not prior to use, but through the very use to which the terms are put. Hence arise an endless crop of misunderstandings and fruitless arguments. Unable to see in language anything but the dictionary meaning of terms, and pinning the pragmatist down to this, we accuse him of all sorts of doctrines which as often as not are the precise opposite of what he wants to convey; we flatter ourselves that we have understood him when as a matter of fact we are not even within sight of his position. We on our side are arguing about the face-values of words; he, on his side, is using these words as pointers, or as doors opening into a concrete whole of experience which contains within itself ten thousand things besides the abstract meaning indicated in the dictionary.[5]

The philosophy of William James, as Jacks further observes, was criticized before it was understood. To understand James, he says, requires "something more than open-mindedness and something more than intellctual acumen . . . it requires a degree of imagination sufficient to carry us into a world where language conveys a set of values certainly other, and perhaps richer, than are implied by the ordinary use of philosophical terms."[6] In the discussion on truth, in particular, James's problem was most acute; and here he and his opponents became deeply involved in verbal difficulties.

While James affirms that the knower, knowledge, and the thing known are all one in the sense that they are all data of experience, he also reaffirms the existence of independent objects—"independent, not of experience, since they *are* experience (or are *as* experienced), but of ideas about them, being a priori condition of the meaning and truth of these ideas."[7] The idea and the reality "form mutually separated parts of a common world of experiences. . . ."[8]

James, who complains frequently about misinterpretations that present him as a subjectivist or idealist, insists that he believes in the existence of objective beings: "I conceive realities as existent, as having existed, or about to exist, in absolute independence of my thought of them."[9] "It seems as if the whole world had conspired to insist that I *shall* not be a realist, in spite of anything I may say I am to the contrary. . . . It seems hard to be accused of thinking what one has never thought, even though one may have seemed in one's clumsiness to say it."[10]

James's position on human knowledge rejects Rationalism (also referred to as Absolutism or Intellectualism), which says that perfect truth now actually exists, and scepticism, which says that there is no conclusive evidence that *anything* is true. James also denies the intellectualist's affirmation that truth now exists ready-made and may now be appropriated by man. His rejection of the rationalist's position, however, does not lead him to scepticism, for he finds the sceptic's fear of making an error as absurd and irrational as the absolutist's belief in the existence now of a body of ready-made truths.

Truth is not the noble, remote reality of the intellectualists, spelled with a capital T, abiding in a glorious trans-empirical realm. Instead, it is a completely indispensable, "practical" element in the maintenance of life; its existence *must* be affirmed for practical reasons, even if no theoretical proof of its being could be found. "The postulate that there is truth, and that it is the destiny of our minds to attain it, we are deliberately resolving to make, though the sceptic will not make it."[11]

Life demands truth, a truth which must not be "outside of the framework of the pragmatic system, outside of that jungle of empirical workings and leadings, and their nearer and ulterior terminations. . . ."[12] Progress has been made in discovering the nature of the truth—by thinkers who have steered clear of dogmatism and positivism and who have remained free from official pretensions. "To me, 'Truth,' if there be any truth," says James, "would seem to exist for the express confusion of this kind of thing [the professional philosophy-shop with all of its pretensions], and to reveal itself in whispers to the 'meek lovers of the Good,' in their solitude, the Darwins, the Lockes, etc., and to be expressly incompatible with officialdom. 'Officials' are products of no deep stratum of experience."[13]

The ranks of those philosophers who have contributed to an understanding of truths include all who have attempted to bring *truth* into a dynamic relationship with life. Such thinkers have tried to have truths respect the dynamic, changing, concrete nature of reality; and they have built a philosophy on their respect for the richness of being and rejected the intellectualist's awe for logic and consistency.

These "meek lovers of the Good" seek clues to the nature of knowledge and of truth wherever such clues may be found—even in the most primitive of settings and the most mundane and practical of situations. In the case of James, *his* clue originated in the biology and psychology of his time—in the teleological interpretation of mind.

I *Teleological Truths*

"The teleological character of mind . . . ," according to Ralph Barton Perry, "may be said to be the germinal idea of James's psychology, epistemology, and philosophy of religion."[14] By embracing the teleological viewpoint in philosophy, James changed the role of mind from that of a disinterested spectator of ready-made existence into that of an "active participant in the shaping of the future."[15] This one change gave, in all departments of his philosophy, a uniquely active role to the human individual by making man a co-creator of the universe and of his own destiny.

Originally, James presented the teleological viewpoint as a psychological theory, with evident indebtedness to Darwin's observations. In his *Talks to Teachers*, for example, the psychological and biological origins were clearly indicated:

. . . in the psychology of our own day the emphasis is transferred from the mind's purely rational function, where Plato and Aristotle, and what one may call the whole classic tradition in philosophy had placed it, to the long neglected practical side. The theory of evolution is mainly responsible for this. Man, we now have reason to believe, has been evolved from infra-human ancestors, in whom pure reason hardly existed, if at all, and whose mind, so far as it can have had any function, would appear to have been an organ for adapting their movements to the impressions received from the environment, so as to escape the better from destruction.[16]

Man, having survived for millennia in difficult environments, must, obviously, have found the means to do so. In this discovery, his mind certainly played major parts. It must have worked out beliefs which led to conduct insuring survival. Man's success points, therefore, to the teleological nature of his mind: "Whatever 'truth' may be 'in itself,' truth *as applicable to life* is what we literally must have, or die":[17]

> . . . those very functions of the mind that do not refer directly to this world's environment, the ethical utopias, aesthetic visions, insights into eternal truth, and fanciful logical combinations, could never be carried on at all by a human individual, unless the mind that produced them in him were also able to produce more practically useful products. The latter are thus the more essential, or at least the more primordial results.[18]

Thus does Semmel in Berlin suggest that no human conception whatever is more than an instrument of biological utility; and that if it be successfully that, we may call it true, whatever it resembles or fails to resemble. Bergson, and more particularly his disciples Wilbois, LeRoy, and others in France, have defended a very similar doctrine. Ostwald, in Leipzig, with his *Energetics,* belongs to the same school, which has received the most thoroughgoingly philosophical of its expressions here in America, in the publications of Professor Dewey and his pupils in Chicago University. . . .[19]

In other words, we are all fated to be *a priori* teleologists whether we will or not. Interests which we bring with us, and simply posit or take our stand upon, are the very flour out of which our mental dough is kneaded. The organism of thought, from the very dawn of discomfort or ease in the polyp to the intellectual joy of Laplace among his formulas, is teleological through and through.[20]

However, man, having survived by the teleological use of ideas, arrived at the stage of philosophizing; and he then displaced the teleological explanation with lofty intellectualisms and rationalisms, far removed from the exigencies of life.

II *Begetting the Truths*

Henri Bergson, in his introduction to the French edition of *Pragmatism*, describes the theory of truth in James's philosophy in illuminating metaphors. He carefully relates the objective nature of reality with the transformations wrought upon it by man, the begettor of truth:

> While for other philosophers truth is a "discovery," for pragmatism it is an "invention." Like any technological device, it depends on the properties of nature, but it is none the less a creation of the human mind. Or, to change the figure, truth is a "route" which man takes in traversing nature: the route must conform to nature, but so far as nature is concerned other routes might equally well have been discovered, laid out, and followed. When the routes are once established they constitute those general characteristics of the human mind which make up common sense, or which philosophers call "the categories."[21]

The truth-seeking man does not approach reality looking for established pre-organized "facts" or "truths," nor does he hope to make exact mental copies of the order that is revealed to him. Instead, he finds experience to be a trackless wilderness that is susceptible to many types of organization; he finds experience merely *capable* of bearing truths. Experience awaits fertilization by man; this fertilization, working upon the formless chaos of experience, creates universes molded by human thoughts, volitions, desires, faiths. Out of the chaos, man begets societies, sciences, arts, philosophies, handicrafts—every articulate form of thought, aspiration, and action. Through man, experience is organized, reorganized, structured, and penetrated with human meanings. Man is that part of reality which adds intelligence to nature.

Although man, in the context of experience, acts as the begettor of truths and displays initiative and originality, he cannot, nevertheless, ignore the objective features of experience. Experience, too, brings certain realities to the truth-begetting process; and these contribute inevitably to the product: " 'Nature' *is* what we make it, but she cooperates in the making, and resists certain attempts. She contains classes and can only be *generalized* in certain ways."[22] "But within our experience *itself*, at any rate, humanism says, some determinations show themselves as being independent of others; some questions if we ever ask them, can only be answered in one way...."[23]

Although man must take into account the objective features of "nature," he must not therefore conclude that these features, important and essential though they be, are the only aspects of reality to be considered in arriving at the "truth." Respect for these aspects should not lead him to deny or minimize the legitimate and essential subjective, human elements which must act in the generation of truths. He must not allow himself to equate truth with the faithful copying or duplication of independent, "objective" realities. Truth is not nature-minus-man's-remodellings, nor man-minus-nature's-coercive-features; truth is actually the offspring of experience fertilized by man.

The doctrine that truth is a ready-made reality, which the human mind discovers, was to James a great *bête noir*.[24] Calling this view at various times Intellectualism, "vicious Intellectualism," Rationalism, or Idealism, he considered this doctrine the most pernicious and insidious product of the "philosophy-shop." The claim that *Truth* was anterior to man and superior to man was idolatrous, for it demanded that man conform to "Truth" regardless of his own needs and interests. Such claims were made in the concrete, James saw, in the scientific or philosophic determinism which rejected man's cherished belief in his own moral responsibility. Thus Intellectualism rejected free will on the grounds of incompatibility with a pre-existing, completely predetermined universe (which in its turn had been conceived by philosophic or quasi-scientific thinking, abstracting from the allegedly inferior parts of which experience is composed). The little "truths" of concrete experience were sacrificed to the great Truth of abstraction.

Idealism, the doctrine that Truth is premade in idealistic form, and Materialism, the doctrine that Truth is premade in materialistic terms, are in eternal enmity with the pragmatic concept of truth. Both Idealism and Materialism spring from the same error —the assumption that truth consists *essentially* in *copying* an existing order. These two brands of "Intellectualism" assume, dogmatically, that "our mind comes upon a world complete in itself, and has the duty of ascertaining its contents; but has no power of re-determining its character, for that is already given."

In attaining truth, man is not to maintain the role of a disinterested spectator; the knower is not a watcher or an observer; *he is an actor*. Knowing is an action; and, like all other types of action, it is done for human ends: "The knower is an actor, and a co-efficient of the truth on one side, while on the other he registers the truth which he helps to create. Mental interests, hypotheses, postulates, so far as they are bases for human action —action which to a great extent transforms the world—help to *make* the truth which they declare."[25] "Truth is *made*, just as health, wealth and strength are made, in the course of experience."[26]

Truth is made in the course of experience in the sense that the knower, unable to attend equally to every part of his experience, selects and organizes those parts which appear most relevant to his interests. He organizes his experiences into a "world," by the process of "selective elimination." "Since the environment to which an organism consciously reacts is the environment as it exists for that organism's consciousness, and since the environment as so viewed is the product of selective elimination on the part of the consciousness concerned, it follows that *conscious selection creates the known world in precisely the same sense in which 'natural selection' creates the species.*"[27]

If the purpose of knowledge were to copy, blindly, the entire panorama of experience, the human species would find its most distinctive character to be a useless, purposeless activity. Correspondence with experience is indeed involved in knowing, but equally involved are the comparison, selection, and suppression of various possibilities and the organization of those possibilities which are selected for their usefulness to man.

Selection and organization are the work of man's power of conceiving or theorizing, and are carried on because of his "indomitable desire to cast the world into more rational shape in our minds than the shape into which it is thrown there by the crude order of experience."[28] This remodelling, done by man's powers of conceiving or theorizing, is effected because of the demands of man's volitional nature, because of "the definite subjective purposes, preferences, fondnesses for certain effects, forms, orders." Without the urgings of these subjective forces, there would not be "the slightest motive" for remodelling "the brute order of our experience." "But as we have the elaborate volitional constitution we do have, the remodelling must be effected; there is no escape."²⁹

This selection and this remodelling act even in so "simple" and elementary an action as the naming of a *thing*. The *thing* itself is an extract from the tremendous flux of experience, carved out of the flux as man carves out constellations; and it is carved to suit some human purposes.³⁰ The *thing* and its relationship to other *things* is, in part, a human invention, or a blaze marked upon some of the trees in the wilderness of pure experience.

This wilderness of pure experience is something man cannot abide in; he must alter it and organize it as soon as possible. The given order of the world is something with which he will have nothing to do except to "get away from it as fast as possible." Man breaks this given order into parts and organizes the units into histories, arts, sciences—then, and only then, has he a world in which he feels "at home."³¹ The realities of his world are an accumulation of his own intellectual inventions,³² just as the realities of his factories are the results of his social and technological inventions. The wonderful thing is not just that man can successfully remodel pure experience but that data lend themselves to that remodelling. This plasticity in the given order is "the miracle of miracles."³³

This responding to man's interests on the part of the crude order of experience is truly extraordinary, as one can readily see if he will consider the range and variety of human interests:

> I cannot stop to argue the point; but I myself believe that all the magnificent achievements of mathematical and physical sciences . . . proceed from our indomitable desire to cast the world into a more rational shape in our minds than the shape into which it is thrown by the crude order of experience. The world has shown itself, to a great extent, plastic to this demand of ours for rationality. How much farther it will show itself plastic no one can say. Our only means of finding out is to try; and I, for one, feel as free to try conceptions of moral as of mechanical or logical rationality. If a certain formula for expressing the nature of the world violates my moral demand, I shall feel as free to throw it overboard, or at least to doubt it, as if it disappointed my demand for uniformity of sequence, for example; the one demand being, so far as I can see, quite as subjective and emotional as the other one is.³⁴

In the great theater of simultaneous possibilities which man confronts and acts in, he chooses those parts of its contents which interest him, and he calls certain ones "essential and lawgiving." These are essential, but as James observes, only *"for our purpose, and our purpose is to conceive simply and to foresee."*[35]

Some of nature's materials respond more slowly than others to man's remodellings; for example, they respond slowly and discouragingly to translation into ethical forms, "but more readily into aesthetic form." The translation into scientific forms is relatively easy and complete. The process of translation will probably never end.[36]

This world in which man moves and lives and has his being, in which he lives by and engenders truths, is the slow, cumulative creation of past generations modified by the remoldings of the present. Man, "by slowly cumulative strokes of choice" has created his world out of the primordial chaos of experience.[37] In this way he has made his world, and he has begotten the truths.

III *Concepts and Percepts: Epistemological Realism*

In reorganizing the primordial chaos of experience, man harnesses perceptual reality in concepts in order to drive it better to his ends. The relationships between concepts and percepts present one of the most difficult and crucial aspects of philosophic thought. Out of its abstruseness have grown the great warring sects—the Realists and the Nominalists, with their dedicated followers and schools and sub-schools.

To James, both concepts and percepts are real, percepts being the more primordial and concepts being derivative and secondary. In man's life, concepts and percepts play indispensable, complementary parts: one provides stability and permanence; the other, his only real contact with the flux of experience.

Concepts, being only *man-made* extracts from the temporal flux, are not to be regarded as "a superior type of being, bright, changeless, true, divine, and utterly opposed in nature to the turbid, restless lower world."[38] The world of change, the world revealed in percepts, is not the mere corruption and falsification of the world of ideas. The perceptual order has its excellences, which are in no way derivative or secondary to concepts. The excellence of both concepts and percepts lies in their *usefulness* to man. Like the two legs by which a man walks, they are each indispensable: who shall say that the *left* leg or the *right* leg does the walking?

To deal successfully with the chaotic flux of experience, man needs some permanent framework or paradigm. Since no permanence can be found in percepts, which are intrinsically transitory, permanence is created by *abstracting* certain experiences from the flux. Man extracts them, confers on them an unchanging nature, and relates them to other concepts in a stable scheme of abstractions. (Some ideas, however, are "necessary." See "Necessary Ideas," Chapter V.)

This stability of concepts is not to be interpreted as a proof that they are anterior or superior to the mutable percepts of human experience. Actually, the stability, which is conferred on concepts for *practical* purposes, is achieved only by stripping the percepts of most of their contents. Abstract concepts have no value except a practical one. "All these are ways of *handling* the perceptual flux and *meeting* distant parts of it; and as far as the primary function of conception goes, we can only conclude it to be what I began by calling it, a faculty superadded to our barely perceptual consciousness for its use in practically adapting us to a larger environment than that of which brutes take account. We *harness* perceptual reality in concepts in order to drive it better to our ends."[39]

The world of concepts and the world of percepts are alike in that both appear at first as a mere chaos of experiences. In both of them, order is introduced by man in terms of the conduct that that order will make possible; the organization and the meaning of each realm are essentially pragmatic: "The serious meaning of a concept, says Mr. Peirce, lies in the concrete difference to some one which its being true will make. Strive to bring all debated conceptions to that 'pragmatic' test, and you will escape vain wrangling: if it can make no practical difference which of two statements be true, then they are really one statement in two verbal forms; if it can make no practical difference whether a given statement be true or false, then the statement has no real meaning."[40]

Thus, if man is interested in obtaining that knowledge which will give him maximum control over nature, he may focus his attention on those percepts and derivative concepts which, when organized, form a scientific world order. In doing so, he will consciously exclude, for his purposes, types of percepts and concepts which are irrelevant, as for example, those related to beauty. In any case, the process of organizing experience in conceptual systems is *practical*—"because all the termini to which we drive are *particular* termini, even when they are facts of the mental order."[41] Conception can occur only for teleological purposes: its practical value lies in showing "the way from a state of things our senses cognize to another state of things our will desires!"[42]

Concepts have no special extra-experiential significance or nature. And they have no claim on man beyond the services which they perform for him: "Use concepts when they help, and drop them when they hinder understanding."[43] Moreover, ". . . however beautiful or otherwise worthy of stationary contemplation the substantive part of a concept may be, the more important part of its significance may naturally be held to be the consequences to which it leads. These may lie either in the way of making us think, or in the way of making us act."[44]

Within man's experiences, these non-perceptual experiences, or concepts, have objectivity as well as subjectivity. Concepts, in their own ways, have reality. Once they have been abstracted from the perceptual flux, they may stand objectively in experience as landmarks, plans, beacons, roads, or goals for action and as objective criteria for evaluating and guiding decisions. Concepts introduce new values into perceptual life and open up wider prospects.

Concepts, however, do *not* exist for their own sakes; they exist to enable man to deal more successfully with the tasks of living his life. They are to be judged, therefore, by the contributions which they make to man in life's various concrete situations. The proper use of concepts brings to the concrete and practical aspects of life "an increase both of vision and power."[45] "Only in so far as they lead us, successfully or unsuccessfully, back into sensible experience again, are our abstracts and universals true or false at all."[46] The significance of the concept is to be seen in its relationship to "perceptual particulars."[47]

Sensation and thought—or perception and conception—are immersed in each other and are indispensable to man and complementary to each other: "The world of common-sense things; the world of material tasks to be done; the world of ethical propositions; the worlds of logic, of music, etc., all abstracted and generalized from long forgotten perceptual instances, from which they have as if it were flowered out, return and merge themselves again in the particulars of our present and future perception. By these *whats* we apperceive all our *thises*."[48]

For James, concepts, with all of their permanence and usefulness, remain ancillary to percepts; his rare expressions to the contrary, containing enthusiastic praise of the role of concepts, refer to the concept as operating as an inspiring ideal in human thought or conduct. In this context the word *ideal* is more appropriate than *idea* or *concept*, as, for example, in the following passage from *Some Problems in Philosophy:* "So strongly do objects that come as universal and eternal arouse our sensibilities, so greatly do life's values deepen when we translate percepts into ideas. The translation appears as far more than the original's equivalent."[49]

What James teaches regarding the nature of concepts is really, as he observes, a somewhat eccentric form of *logical realism*. But his brand of logical realism is different in that it treats concepts as secondary in nature and percepts as primary: "Rationalism," with which logical realism is most often associated, regards concepts as primordial and percepts as secondary. James combines "logical realism with an otherwise empiricist mode of thought."[50]

James insists that percepts be regarded as primordial because of the greater richness and variety which is found in the perceptual flux. The thin, spare concepts, with their sparse contents and rigidly marked-out definitions, are poor relatives of the rich percepts; their meanings are made richer by continually referring them to the perceptual flow. (For example, the concept of civil liberties is enriched, not merely by contemplation, but by plunging it frequently into the perceptual stream where innumerable abuses of civil liberties illuminate the nature of civil rights and broaden the horizons and deepen the meanings of the concept.) Concepts are formed out of the perceptual flux, and James's belief in any theory of "participation" seems generally to say that the concepts participate in the being of the percepts—making the following statement, written in his last years, particularly hard to explain: "What I am affirming here is the platonic doctrine that concepts are singulars, that concept-stuff is inalterable, and that *physical realities are constituted by the various concept-stuffs of which they partake.*"[51]

The problem of how to explain this statement is further aggravated by the fact that it follows twenty-two pages, devoted to an anti-rationalistic exposition on the abuses of concepts, in which James shows that "concepts are secondary formations, inadequate, and only ministerial" and demonstrates that "they falsify as well as omit, and make the flux impossible to understand."[52]

IV *The Abuses of Concepts*

An important corollary of James's Pragmatism and Radical Empiricism is the polemics against what he variously calls "vicious Intellectualism," Rationalism, Absolutism, Platonism. The polemics begin at the outset of his philosophizing when he boldly affirms the freedom of the will against the powerful rationalistic arguments of the determinists, who denounced the "irrationality" represented by freedom in an otherwise consistently pre-ordered universe. The war against intellectualism (*vicious* intellectualism as opposed to *genuine* intellectualism) gained its most widely known, most misunderstood, and most misrepresented slogan in 1806 when James coined the phrase "The Will to Believe" and argued for the rights of feelings and willing against the tyranny of "intellect." Between March, 1909, and the day of his death in August, 1910, he wrote the pages on the abuse of concepts for *Some Problems of Philosophy* and thus continued the warfare to the very end of his life.

Throughout his philosophical career, James denounces the exalting of concepts to the position of tyrannical dictators. Far from sharing the rationalistic admiration for those who peep and botanize on their mothers' graves, James insists upon respecting a *genuine* rationality which takes into account aspects of life other than the purely intellectual. In pursuing his exposition, he attacks the pretensions of the concepts and presents analyses of true rationality, which is discussed later in this chapter. The practical importance of having correct opinions in these matters cannot be overstressed; misuse of concepts introduces the gravest unintelligibilities into our understanding of life; and the consistent acceptance of these unintelligibilities in the practical concerns of life would, if such application were always possible, make living an impossibility.

Concepts have reality and truth, it is true; but only in the way in which a map has reality and truth—as an extract from and guide to the land, lakes, rivers, roads, and other features of reality. But this analogy itself is not adequate because the perceptual flux is not so constant as an earthscape and the concepts are not so passive as a map. The concepts attempt to select, organize, and represent some features of the perceptual flux—but meanwhile the perceptual flux is changing constantly.

The "vicious intellectualists" reject this relatively modest account of the nature and role of the concepts and insist that "the intelligible order ought to supersede the senses rather than interpret them":[53] "The senses, according to this opinion, are organs of wavering illusion that stand in the way of 'knowledge,' in the unalterable sense of that term. They are an unfortunate complication on which philosophers may safely turn their backs."[54]

Conceptual knowledge is never adequate to the fullness of reality: "Reality consists of existential particulars as well as of essences and universals and class-names, and of existential particulars we become aware only in the perceptual flux. *The flux can never be superseded.*"[55] Throughout the process of knowing, man must keep the perceptual flux in mind—if his knowledge is to be constantly in accord with reality. To prove that knowledge must always remain in contact with sensation, James shows that concepts are "secondary formations, inadequate and only ministerial" and that "they falsify as well as omit, and make the flux impossible to understand."[56]

James shows that conception is a secondary process, first, because it is not indispensable to life (and sensation is) and, second, because all conceptual contents originate in the perceptual world: "the famous world of universals would disappear like a soap-bubble if the definite contents of feeling, the *thises* and *thats*, which its terms severally denote, could be at once withdrawn."[57]

Perceptual reality invariably suffers from distortions as a result of conceptual treatment; the perceptual flux is made to appear paradoxical and incomprehensible—and at last it is "proved" to be appearance or illusion. This distortion is the result of two facts:

> First, that when we substitute concepts for percepts, we substitute their relations also. But since the relations of concepts are of static comparison only, it is impossible to substitute them for the dynamic relations with which the perceptual flux is filled. Secondly, the conceptual scheme, consisting as it does of discontinuous terms, can only cover the perceptual flux in spots and incompletely. The one is no full measure of the other, the essential features of the flux escaping whenever we put concepts in its place.[58]

The inadequation between conceptual knowledge and the perceptual flux, which James attributes to the shortcomings of the concepts, is attributed by the rationalists to the imperfections of the perceptual flux. The rationalists consider the concepts more faithful to reality because they and the ultimate reality are static, whereas perceptual life "boils over with activity and change."[59]

V *True Rationality*

Despite the failures of the Rationalists and the failure of the inadequately experimental Empiricism of Hume, James affirms that by a *radical* Empiricism man can attain to genuine rationality. To understand how he can do so, one must make an analysis of experiences to see what constitutes genuine rationality and one must also examine the claims of the various pseudo-rationalisms.

The pseudo-rationalism which has enjoyed the greatest prestige among philosophers is, to James, "intellectualism in the vicious sense." This vicious intellectualism treats of a name as excluding from the fact named "what the name's definition fails positively to include."[60] Intellectualism of this sort began when Socrates and Plato decided that one learns what a thing really is by examining its *definition*. It declares that reality consists of essences which are known when their definitions are known. In James's day, "the vice of intellectualism" was exemplified in Bradley's philosophy wherein "abstract terms are used by him positively excluding all that their definitions fail to include."[61]

Human Knowledge

The prestige of Intellectualism in philosophical circles, especially the prestige of Neo-Hegelianism, was so great in James's day that he found it extremely difficult to make himself understood because the language of idealism and that of radical empiricism, often employing the very same words, have different meanings since they refer to radically different views of reality:

> Nevertheless, if we look on a man's life as it exists, on the life of men that lies in them apart from their learning and science, and that they inwardly and privately follow, we have to confess that the part of it of which rationalism can give an account is relatively superficial. It is the part which has the *prestige* undoubtedly, for it has the loquacity, it can challenge you for proofs, and chop logic, and put you down with words. But it will fail to convince or convert you all the same, if your dumb intuitions are opposed to its conclusions.[62]

When the methods and assumptions of vicious intellectualism lead only into the blind alley of scepticism, the rationalists frantically introduce some *deus ex machina* to save their precious systems. Their face-saving (or thought-saving) activity is vividly described by Gordon Clark: "When the rationalists came to recognize that the real world escapes their neat formulas, they invented unreal worlds from which these stubborn facts were barred. Kant's rational will emigrated to the world of noumena; Bradley escaped contradictions somehow in the Absolute; and Green relied on a transcendent Mind. But this is only to say that human concepts falsify reality."[63] The theorizing mind, having oversimplified its materials, has created voids and disjunctions in its picture of reality and must settle for scepticism or invent some element that fills the voids and joins the fragments to which it had reduced reality. The result, if such inventions are introduced, is some variety of Absolutism, materialistic or idealistic.

However, into the tranquility of these abstract inventions, life and reality are forever bursting, intruding, and disorganizing: "Always things burst by the growing content of experience. Dramatic unities; laws of versification; ecclesiastical systems; scholastic doctrines. Bah! . . . The barbarians are in the line of mental growth, and those who do insist that the ideal and the real are dynamically continuous are those by whom the world is to be saved."⁶⁴

The truly rational, if it is to be found at all, will not be discovered by those who test it exclusively by the demands of intellectualism and abstraction without reference to other equally essential features of knowledge and without reference to willing and feeling. Those who identify the truly rational with that which is consistent within an abstract scheme of things have been deluded by thinking that their preference for stability and consistency is an objective feature of reality. Thinking so, they judge the facts of nature by their theories, instead of judging their theories by the facts which burst in upon them. The truth is not mere abstraction; mere abstraction erects a wall against the truth!

> Essentially it [James's philosophy] protests [says Howard W. Knox] against a severance of "will" from "intelligence," which destroys the intelligibility of both: against the assumption that "everything not imposed upon a will-less and non-cooperant intellect must be counted as false"; a view which James rightly regards as "a preposterous principle which no human being follows in real life" [*Letters* II, 356]. And by recognizing that the impersonal standpoint of science *abstracts from* personality without disposing of it, it breaks down that hard-and-fast barrier between the "subjective" and the "objective" which is the final source of nihilistic scepticism.⁶⁵

In the interests of the truly rational James warred against the misuse of abstraction and tried continually to establish himself in the concrete. In both endeavors he attracted international attention. He tried to thaw out the freezing of the universe produced by centuries of chilling abstractionism and to liberate the living, vibrant objects demobilized under accumulations of ice and snow. At the end of his life he was hailed for "his especial gift to see truth incarnate." Royce declared: "He has lately warned us against thinking of truth as a mere abstraction. And indeed it has always been his especial gift to see truth incarnate —embodied in the truth-seekers. . . ."⁶⁶ In a eulogy in *Revue des Deux Mondes,* Andre Chaumeix also hailed James for restoring life to the universe: ". . . l'univers de William James est libéré de ces notions abstraits. Les faits y ruisselent. C'est un monde vivant . . . un monde charnu qui contraste agréablement avec un univers famélique, décharmé et comme râpé que représent l'école de l'absolu."[67]

For James, the possession of insight into the truly rational required a truth-seeker to cultivate, earnestly, conscious contacts with the concrete in various moments of experience—to see a percept in all its depths and in its manifold relationships with other parts of sensory experience. Herein his philosophic emphasis coincided with that of the great novelists and the Romantic poets. To appreciate and to respect the messages of concrete moments of experience are the first requirements for creating genuine rationality. This appreciation and respect are found, as Ralph Barton Perry observed, in various aspects of James's personality and philosophy: "He had the novelist's interest in character, the dramatist's interest in life, and the poet's interest in nature. In other words, he was repelled by verbalism, logomachy, and abstractness. No philosophy could ultimately satisfy him that did not embrace an intuition of concrete realities. . . ."[68]

The claims of the concrete must not be forgotten as one responds to the desire to create a rational order. This desire for rationality is so strong with some philosophers that, in their eagerness to get away from what does not seem rational, they have grasped whatever seemed most congenial to them, violating at the same time some of the deepest features of reality. If, for example, the philosopher attempts to achieve rationality by emancipating the cognitive faculty from that organic mental whole of which it is but one element, the resulting theory will not receive the "faintest color of plausibility from any fact we can discern."[69]

Man is inclined to accept as rational that which enables him to think "with perfect fluency," that which "lets loose any action which we are fond of exerting," and that which "is such as to define expectancy," thus eliminating mental uneasiness.[70] "An ultimate datum, even though it be logically unrationalized, will, if its quality is such as to define expectancy, be peacefully accepted by the mind; while if it leave the least opportunity for ambiguity in the future, it will to that extent cause mental uneasiness if not distress. Now in the ultimate explanations of the universe which the craving for rationality has elicited from the human mind, the demands of expectancy to be satisfied have always played a fundamental part."[71]

While rationality is recognized in the fact of "unimpeded mental function,"[72] the philosopher must beware of pseudo-rationalities which sacrifice any one or more of the four dimensions of rationality—*the intellectual, the aesthetic, the moral*, and *the practical.*[73] The history of philosophy is full of such pseudo-rationalities which, in satisfying man's desire to have expectancy defined, have rejected essential features of reality. One philosophy after another has failed to attain permanent loyalty because none has completely satisfied the demand for rationality.

All attempts to present the universe as completely rational have failed; and so have all attempts to prove it absolutely irrational. The only alternative lies in the belief that *some* rationality characterizes the universe, and that it co-exists with a vast amount of irrationality. A genuinely rational philosophy must affirm the existence of both the rational and the irrational, both in the external world and in the world within each man. The truly rational philosophy must provide room for both features of reality. In forming philosophical opinions, for example, the philosopher must accept the fact that "the whole man within us," rational and irrational, is at work. "Intellect, will, taste, and passion co-operate just as they do in practical affairs. . . ."[74]

The idealist tradition in philosophy teaches that the unity—or rationality—in the universe is the result of synthetic concepts applied by the intellect. Feelings, regarded as aboriginally discontinuous, are said to be woven together by concepts. This theory is a pseudo-rationalism, which falsely assumes that conception is essentially a unifying process. For James, on the contrary, all concepts are discrete.[75]

The fear of the subjectivity of emotions and will and the reverence for the alleged objectivity of the intellect constitute a two-headed philosophic idol which James attempts to destroy by pointing out that man's contacts with reality are not exclusively intellectual and that the intellectual viewpoints are themselves grounded in subjective preferences and prejudices. The assumption that that world view is best and most objective which excludes man's emotions and will annoyed James constantly. He ridiculed that so-called superior knowledge from which man's subjective preferences had been allegedly purged: "Many persons nowadays seem to think that any conclusion must be very scientific if the arguments in favor of it are all derived from the twitching of frogs' legs—especially if the frogs are decapitated —and that, on the other hand, any doctrine chiefly vouched for by the feelings of human beings—with heads on their shoulders— must be benighted and superstitious."[76]

To attain rationality, a philosophy must take into account in an adequate manner the various coexisting and often competing aspects of nature and of human life. To reduce all reality to one aspect, for example, that intellectualistic aspect which puts the highest value upon consistency, is actually to vote for antirationality. A truly rational philosophy must identify the elements of true rationality and see them as harnessed together working for man's authentic welfare.

> . . . rationality has at least four dimensions, intellectual, aesthetical, moral, and practical; and to find a world rational to a maximal degree *in all these respects simultaneously is no easy matter.* Intellectually, the world of mechanical materialism is the most rational, for we subject its events to mathematical calculation. But the mechanical world is ugly, as arithmetic is ugly, and it is non-moral. Morally, the theistic world is rational enough, but full of intellectual frustrations. The practical world of affairs, in its turn, so supremely rational to the politician, the military man . . . is irrational to moral and artistic temperaments; so that whatever demand for rationality we find satisfied by a philosophic hypothesis, we are liable to find some other demand for rationality unsatisfied by the same hypothesis. The rationality we gain in one coin we thus pay for in another; and the problem accordingly seems at first sight to resolve itself into that of getting a conception which will yield the largest *balance* of perfect rationality of every description.[77]

CHAPTER 5

Truth and Certitude

THE COMMONEST ASSUMPTION with reference to the nature of truth is the belief that the essence of truth is *correspondence* or *copying;* thus a statement is said to be true if it corresponds with the situation or object to which it refers. This almost universal definition of truth James rejects; and, as he does so, he becomes involved in his most subtle and most widely misunderstood arguments. Having shocked many by insisting that truth is "made" by man, he compounds his offense by arguing that the essence of truth is not *correspondence* but *verification:* "The truth of an idea is not a stagnant property inherent in it. Truth *happens* to an idea. It *becomes* true, is *made* true by events. Its verity *is* in fact an event, a process, the process namely of its verifying itself, its veri*fication*. Its validity is the process of its vali*dation*."[1]

I *Truth as Verification*

Truth is not solely or essentially a matter of correspondence. Correspondence exists in innumerable other types of situations, with objects related to objects in special ways, in which the function of truth has no articulate role. Correspondences can exist for eons without reference to any truths; there can be *correspondence* without *truth*.

Truth arrives on the scene when a mind starts to observe, select, and organize and begins to make affirmations about reality. The importance of having statements corresponding faithfully with reality in the knowledge of phenomenal facts leads, unfortunately, to the conclusion that correspondence is *the very essence of truth*. However, as James observes, "To copy a reality is, indeed, one very important way of agreeing with it, but it is far from being essential. The essential thing is the process of being guided."[2]

Truth requires *agreement*. Correspondence means a mere passive copying of the objective reality; agreeing means entering into a dynamic, constructive relationship with reality: "To agree in the widest sense with a reality can only mean to be guided either straight up to it or into its surroundings, or to be put into such working touch with it as to handle either it or something connected with it better than if we disagreed. . . . [any idea] that doesn't entangle our progress in frustrations, that *fits* in fact, and adapts our life to the reality's whole setting will agree sufficiently to meet the requirement. It will be true of that reality."[3]

A so-called truth is tested by its success in getting the thinker into fruitful relationships with various parts of reality. Verification, which is *the* truth of an idea, consists in the "agreeable leading" of the thinker into reality.[4] *"True ideas are those that we can assimilate, validate, corroborate, and verify. False ideas are those that we cannot."*[5]

II Beliefs and Actions

Just as the essence of truth lies in verification, the *act* which is its truth, so the significance of a belief lies in the kind of action which it leads to. "Beliefs . . . are rules for action; and the whole function of thinking is but one step in the production of active habits."[6]

James rejects the notion that belief consists in the static possession of fixed truths, carefully preserved from changes, like data locked in a filing cabinet. Beliefs, relating to a world which is exploding with changes, must retain real connections with that world. They must partake in the changes and they must guide man in his actions in the changing course of experience. They must not merely reflect change, and not merely guide man in dealing with the changes—they must also play an active part in bringing about desirable changes.

To give belief its full reality, James taught that belief was an act of the whole man—not just a function of logic. He saw belief in the total world of man and his environment, and emphasized especially the biological and psychological roles of belief.

[87]

"But [writes Howard Knox] when belief is recognized strictly as a function of the organism, and when we observe that this function is to establish harmonious relations between the organism and the circumambient reality, or environment, it becomes impossible to maintain so simple a distinction between psychology and logic. For belief, taken quite abstractly, simply *qua* belief, has not the slightest biological meaning. Broadly speaking, it is only *true* beliefs that are useful for life."[7]

Whatever beliefs might, or might not, be, it must be insisted that they exist for the sake of action. From whatever source a belief may come, reputable or disreputable, it is to be judged in terms of the actions which rise from it. James defended, against the solemn condemnations of scientific orthodoxy, the rights of faith healers to practice their scientifically "disreputable" approach to health and disease. If their beliefs lead to cures, is this fact to be denied because of prejudices against certain features of those beliefs? By their fruits, not by their roots, shall you know them!

III *The Will to Believe*

The active role of belief is put in a dramatic light when one examines those instances—so crucial in human life—wherein belief *creates* its own verification, that is, contributes essentially to the production of the reality that is believed in. From the psychological point of view, will and belief, meaning a certain relation between objects and the self, are only two names for the same *psychological* phenomenon.[8] Thus, in some instances, the existence of an object depends upon belief and willing.

In the physical realm, the belief that one can jump across the brook or throw the ball through the hoop plays an important part in one's doing so. The belief contributes toward the realization of the physical phenomenon. And in the moral or spiritual realm, one's belief in the potential goodness of a person who is morally derelict in some respect may likewise, by creating a favorable moral climate, contribute to the realization of moral improvements. In both cases, belief generates phenomena which are favorable to the realization of the object believed in. Faith helps create the fact.

This creative role of belief works in such a way that if belief is withheld, the object believed in will not become real. If this

Truth and Certitude

is so, then the intellectualistic insistence that belief be withheld until the logical intellect be completely coerced, until all doubts have been answered, means that the delivery of some objects into reality will never occur.

James defended the lawfulness of voluntarily adopted faith in matters where truths depend on man's personal actions. Here, faith based on desire, he said, is "certainly a lawful and possibly an indispensable thing."[9] In such instances, man is acting, not as a passive portion of the universe, but is displaying "a curious autonomy," as if he were a small active center of action on his own account.[10]

The intellectualistic fear of believing before all of the evidence is "in" proves to be, upon careful analysis, a profoundly irrational approach to life and thought *in the matter of beliefs which make essential differences to life,* for example, the belief that there are or are not moral realities by which man should conduct his life. "Moral scepticism can no more be refuted or proved by logic than intellectual scepticism can. When we stick to it that there *is* truth (be it of either kind), *we do so with our whole nature and resolve to stand or fall by the results.*"[11]

The phenomena of belief are much too complex for the simple rules of the intellectualistic logician. Faced with a *hypothesis,* or proposition for belief, a man discovers that it is either *live* or *dead,* that is, appeals as a real possibility or not. The decision between two hypotheses, called by James an *option,* may be of several kinds: (1) living or dead; (2) forced or avoidable; (3) momentous or trivial. A *genuine option* faces a knower when the option is *forced, living,* and *momentous.*[12]

To Americans of James's day, the choice between being a Hindu or a Mohammedan would probably be a dead option, but that between being an agnostic or a Christian a living one. The choice between going out with or without one's umbrella is a genuine option, but not forced; however, a dilemma based upon "a complete logical disjunction, with no possibility of not choosing," such as "Either accept this truth or go without it," is a forced option.[13] Finally, an option is momentous if it refers to a unique opportunity not likely ever to be offered again. "He who refuses to embrace a unique opportunity loses the prize as surely as if he tried and failed."[14]

Faced with an option which is *living, forced,* and *momentous,* a man will find that he must make a decision (or postpone his decision, which may have the same practical effects) whether he wishes to or not. In a critical illness, he might find the option of calling in a physician or a Christian Science practitioner to be a living, forced, and momentous choice. To be guided by the physician or the practitioner (or neither) is a choice that cannot wait until all the evidence for orthodox medical practice or for faith healing has been assembled and evaluated. He may decide for the physician or practitioner—a decision made in the absence of complete evidence; or he may decide to reject both of them—this decision is made in the absence of complete evidence. Whatever decision he finally comes to will, in the last analysis, proceed from forces in his life which are other than logical.

"In truths dependent on our personal action . . . faith based upon desire is certainly a lawful and possibly an indispensable thing."[15] For example, in the question of accepting a religious faith, a man should understand that whether he decides for the religious view of life or for the materialistic one, he is in both cases basing his decision on his *desires* for a particular type of world:

> To preach scepticism to us as a duty, until "sufficient evidence" for religion be found, is tantamount therefore to telling us, when in the presence of the religious hypothesis, that to yield to our fear of its being error is wiser and better than to yield to our hope that it may be true. It is not intellect against passion, then; it is only intellect with one passion laying down its law. And by what, forsooth, is the supreme wisdom of that passion warranted? Dupery for dupery, what proof is there that dupery through hope is so much worse than dupery through fear? I, for one, can see no proof; and I simply refuse obedience to the scientist's command to imitate his kind of option, in a case where my own stake is important enough to give me the right to choose my own form of risk.[16]

. . . .

> The thesis I defend is, briefly stated, this: *Our passional nature not only lawfully may, but must, decide an option between propositions, whenever it is a genuine option that cannot by its nature be decided on intellectual grounds; for to say, under such circumstances, "Do not decide, but leave the question open," is itself a passional decision . . . and is attended with the same risk of losing the truth.*[17]

IV Certitude

Although men *must* believe some things to be true and direct their actions accordingly, it does not necessarily follow that they may claim a high degree of certitude regarding their beliefs. As a matter of fact, knowledge most often lacks absolute certitude—because of the limitations of the knower and because of the constantly changing character of the universe. The search for truth, nevertheless, continues; it receives support from man's faith in the reality of the present moment of experience and from the certitude found in *necessary ideas*.

Apart from these two areas of certitude, however, the knower must be satisfied with less than certainty and must stand always ready to revise and rethink what now appears to be positively true. Progress in knowledge is dependent upon accumulating and evaluating more and more experiences and upon rejecting or revising those beliefs which do not fit into the growing body of experience. Knowledge at any one point of time means only the most reliable knowledge *then available:* "I live, to be sure, by the practical faith that we must go on experiencing and thinking over our experience, for only thus can our opinions grow more true; but to hold any one of them—I absolutely do not care which—as if it never could be reinterpreted or corrigible, I believe to be a tremendously mistaken attitude."[18] "But the safe thing is surely to recognize that all the insights of creatures of a day like ourselves must be provisional. The wisest of critics is an altering being, subject to the better insight of the morrow, and right at any moment, only 'up to date' and 'on the whole.' "[19]

This contention that the present truth should be regarded as corrigible does not spring from any perverse delight in intellectual instability but from a healthy fear of losing the truth by the pretension of already possessing it wholly. More and more truth can be gained by adding, revising, and correcting.[20] To regard our present truths as *reasonably probable* is the best attitude for men who believe in the existence of truths and hope for genuine progress in knowledge. Verification comes only in the completed experience of the entire human race; meanwhile, reasonable probability must suffice for guidance in matters such as questions of morality and religion. "Certitude" has been shown not to exist—shown by philosophers, evolutionists, and scientists.

But *truth,* in the form of probability adequate to the needs of life, has survived the demise of certitude as an actual possession of man.

> But three influences have at last conspired to dissolve away this appearance of absoluteness in such facts and theories as we can formulate. First, the philosophical criticisms like those of Mill, Lotze, and Sigwart have emphasized the incongruence of the forms of our thinking with the "things" which the thinking nevertheless successfully handles. (Predicates and subjects, for example, do not live separately in things, as they do in our judgements of them.) Second, not only has the doctrine of evolution weaned us from fixities and inflexibilities in general, and given us a world all plastic, but it has made us ready to imagine almost all our functions, even the intellectual ones, as "adaptations," and possibly transient adaptations, to human needs. Lastly, the enormous growth of the sciences in the past fifty years has reconciled us to the idea that "not quite true" is as near as we can ever get.[21]

Knowledge which possesses certitude that is less than absolute is sufficient for human needs—if it is reinforced by faith. The insistence upon holding out for absolute certitude, being basically an irrational demand, should be regarded as a weakness of human nature from which man must, if he can, free himself.

The rationality of freeing oneself from the false ideal of absolute certitude is shown when one considers that men have never agreed upon any concrete test of what is really true.[22] Absolute objective certitude as an ideal loses its appeal when one sees that theories, far from being revelations or "gnostic answers to some divinely instituted world-enigma," are actually *instruments,* "mental modes of *adaptation* to reality."[23] "If *we* claim only reasonable probability, it will be as much as men who love the truth can ever at any given moment hope to have within their grasp."[24]

V *Necessary Ideas*

How does a reader reconcile the following statements, both truly typical of James's views on knowledge and at the same time apparently contradictory? First, "Objective evidence and certitude are doubtless very fine ideals to play with, but where on this moonlit and dream-visited planet are they found? I am, therefore, myself a complete empiricist so far as my theory of human knowledge goes."[25] Second, "It is a familiar truth that some propositions are *necessary*."[26]

As a matter of fact, James does discover *necessity* in the structure of certain ideas, and with respect to this necessity he can find no possible doubts. Herein he remains *empirical* in the sense that he *discovers* such ideas with this special kind of necessity in the psychology of man; he affirms what he finds, even though these findings cannot be made to fit coherently into the patterns revealed by other types of experience. The necessity in the ideas is a feature of the ideas themselves and depends only on their nature. To be such an idea is to have certain necessities. In the minds of men, these ideas are found, and the necessities of these ideas are revealed.

Certain things are *necessarily* true of a particular "necessary" idea—whereas the truths of other types of ideas—the present blueness of the sky over New York—is *not* necessary. "Where a result comes [with reference to *necessary ideas*], it is due exclusively to the *nature* of the ideas and of the operation. Take blueness and yellowness, for example. We can operate on them in some ways, but not in other ways. We can compare them; but we cannot add one to or subtract it from the other. We can refer them to a common kind, color; but we cannot make one a kind of the other or infer one from the other."[27]

The necessary and eternal relations characteristic of certain ideas are not to be regarded as derived from the percepts in space and time associated with the conceptions. Thus, certain necessary features of aesthetic ideals cannot be explained as derived from aesthetic experiences furnished in the temporal and spatial order. Nor can the accumulated experiences of the human race explain them any more than can the perceptual experiences of an individual; the necessary or *a priori* judgments stand independent of all experiences of a space-and-time nature. In man's thought one finds relations which do much more than repeat the couplings of external experiences.[28] The *inward fitness* of such relations has its own intrinsic originality.

> The world of aesthetics and ethics is an ideal world, a Utopia, *a world which the outer relations persist in contradicting*, but which we as stubbornly persist in striving to make actual. Why do we thus invariably crave to alter the given order of nature? Simply because other relations among things are far more interesting to

us and more charming than the mere rates of frequency of their time- and space-conjunctions. These other relations are all secondary and brain-born, "spontaneous variations" most of them, of our sensibility, whereby certain elements of our experience, and certain arrangements in time and space, have acquired an agreeableness which otherwise would not have been felt. It is true that habitual arrangements may also become agreeable. But this agreeableness of the merely habitual is felt to be a mere ape and counterfeit of real inward fitness; and one sign of intelligence is never to mistake one for the other.[29]

Here, in the realm of necessary ideas man encounters genuine absolutes. These absolutes are *grounded* in experience and constantly *verified* and *re-verified* in the accumulating experiences of mankind. They differ from the pseudo-absolutes of Plato and the other philosophical absolutists in that they are entirely experiential; they require no ground or explanation of an extra-experiential nature. They are absolutes simply and solely because of their own natures. They are not explicable in terms of any external reality—the World of Ideas, the funded experiences of the human race, or the feeling of "rightness" which arises from habitual experiences.

> The moral principles which our mental structure engenders are quite as little explicable *in toto* by habitual experiences having bred inner cohesions. Rightness is not *mere* usualness, wrongness not *mere* oddity, however numerous the facts which might be invoked to prove such identity.[30]
>
> . . . .
>
> No more than higher musical sensibility can the higher moral sensibility be accounted for by the frequency with which outer relations have cohered. Take judgements of justice or equity, for example. Instinctively, one judges everything differently, according as it pertains to one's self or to some one else. Empirically one notices that everybody else does the same. But little by little there dawns in one the judgement "nothing can be right for me which would not be right for another similarly placed"; or "the fulfillment of my desires is intrinsically no more imperative than that of anyone else's" . . . and forthwith the whole mass of the habitual gets overturned. It gets *seriously* overturned only in a few fanatical heads. But its overturning is due to a back-door and not to a front-door process.[31]

Truth and Certitude

The process whereby necessary ideas come to a man is indeed a process of experience, but it differs significantly from the way in which other types of experience arise. To explain this difference, James points out that nature has many ways of producing the same effect: "She may make our ears ring by the sound of a bell, or by a dose of quinine; . . . fill us with terror of certain surroundings by making them really dangerous, or by a blow which produces a pathological alternation of our brain. . . . *In the one case the natural agents produce perceptions which takes cognizance of the agents themselves; in the other case, they produce perceptions which take cognizance of something else.*"[32]

"Experience" in the common meaning of that word refers to perceptions which take cognizance of the agents themselves: seeing a sunset, feeling a moist fog, or hearing a whisper. Here the objects which stimulate the senses become also the object known to consciousness.

The origin of the necessary ideas cannot, of course, be explained in this manner since they do not correspond to any "external" objects. Of one thing we can be sure—*necessary ideas do exist*. On this important point James agrees with the apriorists, but he disagrees with them in contending for a naturalistic view of the *cause* of such ideas.

James favors the view that necessary ideas arose first as "congenital variations, 'accidental' in the first instance, but then transmitted as fixed features of the race."[33] He thinks that they probably occurred first as morphological accidents, as inward summation of effects, rather than as a result of the sensible presence of objects. He asks: "Why may they not, in short, be pure *idiosyncrasies,* spontaneous variations, fitted by good luck (those of them which have survived) to take cognizance of objects (that is, to steer us in our active dealings with them), without being in any intelligible sense immediate derivatives from them?"[34]

The necessary ideas have an extraordinary sort of relationship toward the knowledge which is derived by "ordinary" experience from the world of space and time. Not being derived from such ordinary experience, the necessary ideas operate in their own special ways. Here, "instead of experience engendering the 'inner relations,' the inner relations, are what engender the experience. . . ."³⁵ *"There are then ideals and inward relations amongst the objects of our thought which can in no intelligible sense whatever be interpreted as reproductions of the order of outward experience.* In the aesthetic and ethical realms they conflict with its order—the early Christian with his kingdom of heaven . . . will tell you that the existing order must perish, root and branch, ere the true order can come."³⁶

The independence of the ethical and aesthetic order, for example, is shown thus by the frequent opposition between the ideals expressed in those orders and the facts revealed in experience in space and time. The facts never quite measure up to the ideals, and so one concludes that the ideals do not copy or originate from the facts.

Facts, originating as they do in time-and-space experience, are handled as data for translation into the rational order. The mind, with its consciousness of judgments of subsumption and logic (none of which could have originated in the order of space-and-time experience) constantly seeks to translate the "empirical" order of things into their rational order because the intellect finds the latter more congenial. "Any classification of things into kinds . . . is a more rational way of conceiving the things than is that mere juxtaposition or separation of them as individuals in time and space which is the order of their crude perception."³⁷

> There is . . . a large body of *a priori* or intuitively necessary truths. As a rule, these are truths of *comparisons* only, and in the first instance they express relations between merely mental terms. Nature, however, acts as if some of her realities were identical with those mental terms. So far as she does this, we can make *a priori* propositions concerning natural fact. The aim of both science and philosophy is to make the identifiable terms more numerous. So far it has proved easier to identify nature's things with mental terms of the mechanical than with mental terms of the sentimental order.³⁸

The dignity of those *a priori*, necessary truths—like that of all other types of truths—lies in their usefulness to man in promoting his welfare. Unlike Plato's *a priori* Ideas, which enjoy the higher perfections of the World of Ideas, these necessary ideas of William James have no extra-experiential origins or

Truth and Certitude

connections and are in no degree intrinsically superior to other types of truth. Of human origin, they are of value only in so far as they play useful roles in human life. In these useful roles, the necessary ideas provide standards, ideals, means of classification and of subsumption. They introduce new directions into the time-and-space experiences, but without such experiences the necessary ideas themselves would have no significance. Here, too, this type of knowledge is to be evaluated by pragmatic standards.

CHAPTER 6

Philosophy of Religion

THE FULLEST EXPRESSION of William James's philosophy of religion is found in his classical volume *The Varieties of Religious Experience,* which he significantly subtitled *A Study in Human Nature.* Originally prepared for delivery as the Gifford Lectures on Natural Religion at the University of Edinburgh, this work presents nevertheless only a limited aspect of James's thinking on the subject of religion. In this series of lectures, which delighted his enthusiastic audiences at Edinburgh and later inspired generations of readers, James examined man's religious constitution or appetite for religion, with special emphasis on extraordinary cases of religious experiences.

He expressed hope that he would be able to write a companion volume on the *metaphysical* aspects of religion in which he would show how the religious appetites are satisfied. Unfortunately, ill health, other duties, and his death within seven years of the publication of *The Varieties* blocked the realization of this hope. But in other works, written in the remaining years of his life, his expressed views on the philosophy of religion show the outlines of his thoughts sufficiently so that one can tell what he might have said about God and man in such a volume.

In his views on the philosophy of religion, James reveals those dominant currents of thought and personality which shape his work in every realm of philosophy: his profound concern for the human individual and for all the aspects of man's personality which shape his work in every realm of philosophy; his concern for the reality of the *concrete* experience and his unwillingness to toady to abstractions, regardless of their prestige in the views of the materialists, absolutists, or orthodox theists; his conviction

Philosophy of Religion

that the highest significance of a belief lay in the moral actions which it led to; his belief that both knowledge and the universe are constantly taking on new realities, growing and expanding constantly; his conviction that evil is *real* and that man's most significant challenge lies in fighting it.

His own personality, too, enters here, quite unapologetically, into the formulation of his views. His sense of humor, his impatience with pretense or academic arrogance, and his rejection of trifling, sneering attitudes toward life—all make his philosophy of religion independent, melioristic, and profoundly challenging.

I *James's Personal Religious Life*

James's own religious life began with his religious formation in the extremely devout and extremely heterodox household of his prophet father, and then moved through a period of naturalism when, as a young student of science (about 1863), he reacted against traditional theism. Until 1870 James accepted, quite unhappily, the naturalistic hypothesis. In that year, the already mentioned profound crisis in his life, brought on by the deterministic hypothesis that man has no moral freedom, led him into despair; but philosophy, through the works of Renouvier, gave him "the courage to think and believe his way out."[1] His way out was a religious and philosophical avenue.

James declared that, far from ever having had a mystical experience, he actually found it impossible to pray; but he envied those gifted to do so. In 1904, he expressed his personal position very clearly:

> My personal position is simple. I have no living sense of commerce with a God. I envy those who have, for I know the addition of such a sense would help me immensely. The Divine, for my *active* life, is limited to abstract concepts which, as ideals, interest and determine me, but do so but faintly, in comparison with what a feeling of God might effect, if I had one. It is largely a question of intensity, but differences of intensity may make one's whole centre of energy shift. Now, although I am so devoid of *Gottesbewustsein* in the directer and stronger sense, yet there is *something in me* which *makes response* when I hear utterances made from that lead by others. I recognize the deeper voice. Something tells me, *"thither lies the truth"*—and I am *sure* it is

not old theistic habits and prejudices of infancy. Those are Christian; and I have grown so out of Christianity that entanglements therewith on the part of a mystical utterance has to be abstracted from and overcome, before I can listen. Call this, if you like, my mystical *germ*. It is a very common germ. It creates the rank and file of believers.[2]

Without this "mystical *germ*," the only position open to a man would be dogmatic, atheistic naturalism. However, says James, "Once allow the mystical germ to influence our beliefs, and I believe that we are in my position."[3] In 1904, in responding to a questionnaire on the subject of religious beliefs, James declared that he believed that God is a combination of Ideality and final efficacy, a person in so far as He must be cognizant and responsive in some way. He asserted that his belief in God was not based on formal, logical arguments for His existence, but upon the *need* which he experienced for such a being and upon the authority of the whole tradition of religious people. He thought of God as a powerful ally of his own ideals, but not as real as an earthly friend. While he has never felt God's presence directly, he has "a germ of something similar" in him which forces him to respect the testimony of those who claim to have had such a type of experience. The Bible he finds all too human to be accepted as *authority* in religious matters: "It is so human a book that I don't see how belief in its divine authority can survive the reading of it."

God, he declares, is not the *only* spiritual reality to be believed in: "Religion means primarily a universe of spiritual relations surrounding the earthly practical ones, not merely relations of 'values,' but agencies and their activities. I suppose that the chief premise for my hospitality towards the religious testimony of others is my conviction that 'normal' or 'sane' consciousness is so small a part of actual experience. What e'er be true, it is not true exclusively, as philistine scientific opinion assumes. The other kinds of consciousness bear witness to a much wider universe of experiences, from which our belief selects and emphasizes such parts as best satisfy our needs."[4]

In his role as a professor at Harvard, James publicly expressed his faith by attending services at the university chapel on every day on which he taught classes. For this example to the students he was hailed at the time of his death in the columns of a news-

Philosophy of Religion

paper: "Profoundly religious by nature and by conviction, William James was one of the most constant attendants at Harvard Chapel during his long term of active service as teacher. Along with the late Prof. Shaler, also a great humanist, he did much to show to the undergraduate world that scholarship and modernity were not inconsistent with worship and attendance on discussion of spiritual things."[5]

Within William James—medical doctor, scientist, psychologist, philosopher—still ran the strong religious currents of his prophet father and devout Presbyterian grandfather. William's faith, most often controlled and channeled in careful expositions, sometimes broke out in lyrical appreciations of the lives of the saints. He was, as J. Hartley Grattan says, "animated by an intensely religious aspiration even while not possessing a religious personality himself. He was predominantly a moralist and with a religious bent—an ethical theist."[6]

The wisest and most perceptive insights into the spiritual life of James were probably those of his friend John Jay Chapman (although Chapman, unfortunately, failed to appreciate his greatness as a *thinker*):

> The fear with which his mind was tinctured was the very vice of which I should accuse the Ethical Society—a fear of the symbols of religion. His heart had been a little seared by early terror. The intellectual part of him was enfeebled by the agnosticism of 1870.[7]
>
> . . . .
>
> The great religious impulse at the back of all his work, and which pierces through at every point, never became expressed in conclusive literary form, or in dogmatic utterance. It never became formulated in his own mind into a stateable belief. And yet it controlled his whole life and mind, and accomplished a great work in the world. The spirit of the priest was in him—in his books and in his conversation. He was a sage, and a holy man; and everybody put off his shoes before him . . . had the process [of rapid intensification] continued much longer, the mere sight of him must have moved beholders to amend their lives.[8]
>
> . . . .
>
> There has recently been an age of agnosticism; it is closing. An age of faith is in progress. The Desert of Agnosticism has been crossed; and some of those leaders who helped multitudes to pass across it, were destined not to enter the promised land them-

selves. Such men are ever among the greatest of their generation. I am thinking of William James, who was in himself more than he either saw or thought. At the time he was writing I saw in him only the ineffectual thinker, but later I came to see in him the saint.[9]

II A Pragmatic and Empirical Approach

James's approach to the philosophy of religion, in line with his general approach to philosophic problems, is characteristically pragmatic and empirical. One discovers what religion really is by examining the experiences of religious persons, all the while being careful to eliminate one's own *a priori* notions. The values of religious phenomena are discovered by examining the effects which they produce; for, in terms of *pragmatic* criteria, these and all other phenomena can be rightly judged only by their fruits.

With James, the pragmatic approach to the philosophy of religion is dominated by ethical considerations; in fact, James approaches religious experiences and theology *by way of ethics*. What is desirable and what is true in religion are determined by examining the moral fruits of various religious practices and beliefs. Thus it is perfectly true, as Julius Seelye Bixler observes, "that the threads of his philosophy converge at one point into a defense of religious faith, and that *his ethics and his purposive view of human life lead him to belief in a Deity*."[10]

In his philosophizing about religion, James, with an open and observant mind, examined the phenomena of religious experiences; here he formulated a rational alternative to the "scientific" and "religious" *proofs* of Predestination which, as Howard Knox declares, "had been held up for our admiration as the necessary goal of enlightened Reason."[11] In James's philosophy of religion, as elsewhere, John Cowper Powys's observation is vindicated: "Alas! There are few modern philosophers as liberated from both rationalistic and religious prejudice as the late incomparable William James."[12] Free from the preconceptions of materialism and absolute idealism, and detached from loyalty to any ecclesiastical dogmas, James could and did face the data of religious experiences with objective openmindedness; and he responded to them with profound sensitivity.

III The Nature of Religious Experience

What *is* religion? The word *religion* does not stand for any single principle or entity, and religion has many characters which may in turn be equally important. Therefore, any abstract conception which must single out some one entity and eliminate all others is misleading. Instead of being seduced into the theorizing fallacy of seeking a definition as the key to the nature of religion, one should inquire into its various meanings in human experience. Thus religion has its external aspects, with worship, sacrifice, theology, ceremonies, and ecclesiastical organizations. It is also, in a more personal way, the inner dispositions of man "which form the centre of his interest, his conscience, his deserts, his helplessness, and his incompleteness."[13]

James, in *The Varieties of Religious Experience* and elsewhere, generally considers religion only in its personal aspect, believing that this is more fundamental than theologies or ecclesiasticisms: "Churches, when once established, live at second hand upon tradition; but the *founders* of every church owed their power originally to the fact of their direct personal communion with the divine. Not only the superhuman founders, the Christ, the Buddha, Mahomet, but all the originators of Christian sects have been in this case;—so personal religion should still seem the primordial thing, even to those who continue to esteem it incomplete."[14]

The meaning of religion, as one should generally understand it throughout James's writings, is succinctly described in *The Varieties* in the following *concrete* terms: "Religion, therefore, as I now ask you arbitrarily to take it, shall mean for us *the feelings, acts, and experiences of individual men in their solitude, so far as they apprehend themselves to stand in relation to whatever they may consider the divine.* Since the relation may be either moral, physical, or ritual, it is evident that out of religion in the sense in which we take it, theologies, philosophies, and ecclesiastical organizations may secondarily grow."[15]

The *divine* to which men find themselves related in their religious feelings, acts, and experiences may be any object that is god*like*, whether it be a concrete deity or not.[16] Thus, Emerson in his relationships with the universe's divine soul must be said to have had religious experiences, even though his divine was not a deity in the usual sense of the word. It *was* god*like*, however, in the sense that it could be trusted "to protect all ideal interests and keep the world's [moral] balance straight."[17]

Religion refers to man's total reaction upon life. Such reactions must be serious and grave rather than pert: "There must be something solemn, serious, and tender about any attitude which we denominate religious. If glad, it must not grin or snicker; if sad, it must not scream or curse. . . . The divine shall mean for us only such a primal reality as the individual feels impelled to respond to solemnly and gravely, and neither by a curse nor a jest."[18] Where a religion regards the world as tragic, the tragedy must be understood as purging; religious sadness, wherever it exists, must possess a purgatorial note.

Individual churches and religious traditions differ widely with respect to the manner in which they propose that men accept the universe. Thus, in comparing the "passionate happiness of Christian saints" with the "drab discolored way of stoic resignation to necessity," one discovers "two discontinuous psychological universes."[19] The difference is more than doctrinal; it is a difference of emotional moods which sets, for example, the convinced Stoic apart from the devout Christian. Where the Stoic accepts and respects the *animus mundi* in a dispassionate manner, the ideal Christian literally abounds in agreement and "runs out to embrace the divine decrees."[20] The genuine Christian shares the boundless enthusiasm of Mary Moody Emerson, who declared, "Let me be a blot on this fair world, the obscurest, the loneliest sufferer, with one proviso,—that I know it is His agency. I will love Him though He shed frost and darkness in every way of mine."[21] The Christian's enthusiasm transforms passive acceptance of the universe into delight; it converts the heavy burden of righteousness into a pleasure—because it is borne out of love for a Heavenly Father, who cares for His children.

For James, the power of religion to transform duty into an enthusiastic temper of espousal was the most practical meaningful feature of the religious life. For him, this transformation was a *new reach of freedom for man;* in it, man perceived "the keynote of the universe" sounding in his ears.[22] It was undoubtedly regarded by James as the highest dimension of human experience.

IV Religion, Faith, and Feelings

Against the assertions that religious beliefs could not be proved by intellectual means and that such beliefs therefore must be accepted by rational men, James argues that faith can be legitimately accepted on other grounds just as trustworthy as the intellect. Man's feelings and needs, he declares, just as much as man's intellect, are indicative of the nature of things. Arguing for the legitimacy of the roles of feelings and needs as indicators of religious truths, James declares to his Hibbert Lectures audience that he was "bent on rehabilitating the element of feeling in religion and subordinating its intellectual part."[23]

What impressed James most about knowledge was its constructive, practical powers, and so it was perfectly in accord with his general theory of knowledge for him to see religious belief not just as a report on existing realities but also, in certain respects, as a creative force which brings about its own verification: "faith acts on the powers above him as a claim, and creates its own verification."[24] He observed that "my willingness to run the risk of acting as if my personal need of taking the world religiously might be prophetic and right."[25]

> Now the metaphysical and religious alternatives are largely of this kind. We have but this one life in which to take up our attitudes towards them, no insurance company is there to cover us, and if we are wrong, our error, even though it be not as great as the old hell-fire theology pretended, may yet be momentous.[26]
>
> . . . .
>
> To preach scepticism to us as a duty until "sufficient evidence" for religion be found, is tantamount therefore to telling us, when in presence of the religious hypothesis, that to yield to our fear of its being error is wiser and better than to yield to our hope that it may be true. It is not intellect against all passions, then; it is only intellect with one passion laying down its law.[27]

The "passion" which lays down the law for the intellect when it casts its vote for scepticism in matters of religion is the *passion of fear*—fear of being in error. The "passion" which directs the intellect to vote for faith is *hope*—hope that the truth will be found to correspond with man's religious aspirations and feelings. In either case, the outcome is based on emotions; and the intellectual snobbery of the sceptic in his contempt for faith has, in the final analysis, a basis which is also emotional.

Which hypothesis will turn out to be true, that of religion or that of scepticism, can be seen only by examining the kind of results produced by acting on them. James believes that the practical results engendered by religious faith are superior to those produced by scepticism. Faith produces the superior results—and is therefore "true": "It may be true that work is still doing in the world-process, and that in that work we are called to bear our share. The character of the world's results may in part depend upon our acts. Our acts may depend on our religion,—on our not-resisting our faith-tendencies, or on our sustaining them in spite of 'evidence' being incomplete. These faith-tendencies in turn are but expressions of our good-will towards certain forms of result."[28]

In the matter of religious faith, as in some other matters, the "truth" of a "fact" is partly determined by the creative participation of the individual. The quality and the nature of such participation are in turn determined by feelings, temperament, and mental powers, which can operate effectively only in response to an "unreasoned and immediate assurance . . . the deepest thing in us." Compared with this assurance, "reasoned argument is but a surface exhibition. Instinct leads, intelligence does but follow."[29]

Emphasis upon the intellectual arguments for the validity of religious beliefs, if it involves the belittling of the emotional dimensions of life, must be viewed as another disastrous surrender to the forces of "vicious" intellectualism. As a matter of fact, the emotions play a major part in religious faith, and emotional enlargement and liberation of the personality are among the most distinctive features of the faith-state. This flowering of the emotions, judged in terms of the fruits which it bears, provides ample "proof" for the validity of religious beliefs.

The intellectual formulations and "proofs," so much insisted upon by pseudo-intellectualism are, as a matter of fact, only very poor substitutes for the concrete emotions associated with the religious life: "I do believe that feeling is the deeper source of religion, and that philosophic and theological formulas are secondary products, like translations into another tongue."[30] The religious feelings—hope, joy, altruistic love—are not, however, in themselves or in their fruits, to be regarded *merely* as a means for proving the validity of religious claims. Much more importantly, they must be seen as "an absolute addition to the Subject's range of life," giving him "a new sphere of power."[31] This new range of life enables the religious man to renounce joyfully his selfish interests in favor of the service of man and God; it opens up otherwise unobtainable spiritual resources which nourish and refresh him throughout every day of his life.

In this area of feelings, and not in the area of theory and intellection, the religious men of all faiths find agreement. "When we survey the whole field of religion, we find a great variety in the thoughts that have prevailed there; but the feelings on the one hand and the conduct on the other are almost always the same, for Stoic, Christian, and Buddhist saints are practically indistinguishable in their lives."[32] From this one can conclude that *feelings and conduct, not theories, are the essence of religious life:*

> The theories which Religion generates, being thus variable, are secondary; and if you wish to grasp her essence, you must look to the feelings and the conduct as being the more constant elements. It is between these two elements that the short circuit exists on which she carries on her principal business, while the ideas and symbols and other institutions form loop-lines which may be perfections and improvements, and may even some day all be united into one harmonious system, but which are not to be regarded as organs with an indispensable function, necessary at all times for religious life to go on.[33]

The world of *spiritual* reality is open only to those individuals who *desire* such a reality, just as the world of *moral* reality is real only for those who in their hearts want such a world: "If your heart does not *want* a world of moral reality, your head will assuredly never make you believe in one. Mephistophelian scepticism, indeed, will satisfy the head's play-instincts much better than any rigorous idealism can."[34]

The importance of desire and emotions in relation to the

faith-state is demonstrated in the lives of those religious persons who have very little in the way of intellectual apprehension of religion but a great deal of religiously oriented emotions. "The faith-state may hold a very minimum of intellectual content. . . . It may be a mere vague enthusiasm, half spiritual, half vital, a courage, and a feeling that great and wondrous things are in the air."[35] These feelings and the good works which they inspire require no buttressing by intellectual "proofs": to deny the validity of the faith-state because of the absence of "proofs" is to indulge in another absurdity of vicious intellectualism.

The *believing heart* has authority which one man may accept just as another may, for reasons of temperament, accept instead the authority of the head-minus-the-heart. This believing heart has its own reasons, as Pascal asserted: "Le coeur a ses raisons, que la raison ne connait pas." Life is more fundamental than reason or logic, and *"beliefs grow directly out of the needs of life and furnish the basis for arguments instead of depending on them."*[36]

James shows that the faith-state actually involves faith, will, future verification, the empirical approach, subjective convictions, and temperamental passional decisions. And he is, of course, making applications of his general theories about knowledge, particularly those set forth in "The Will to Believe." Religious faith and belief in a moral order are postulated to satisfy man's deepest demands, but in these types of beliefs, based as they are on moral postulates instead of on sense experience, the *creative* element of belief is especially active. The belief in God, however, as Bixler points out, has a unique aspect:

> The belief in God, however, has another side. We may approach God by an act of will, but God on his part stoops to our weakness. In the essays published with *The Will to Believe* James had said that our power of moral and volitional response is probably our deepest organ of communication with the nature of things [141]. But in the *Varieties* the deepest organ of communication is the passive experience [381], the experience of reconciliation [388], when man feels the touch of a Power greater than himself, and when instead of selecting and creating his own reality, he is content to contemplate the Ideal as presented, finding in it a new authority and a new source of strength.[37]

V Once-born and Twice-born Souls

The history of religion reveals a profound cleavage between religions: on the one hand are those which may be called the religions of purely natural man and on the other those which may be described as the religions of the "twice-born" man. Christianity, Judaism, Mohammedanism, Buddhism are examples of religions which insist upon the "death" of the natural man and his "rebirth" into the godly world of faith. Stoicism and Epicureanism marked the conclusion of the "once-born" period in religion and represent the highest flights of the purely natural man.[38] This latter type of religion calls for continued living on a "natural" plane, but the other demands a rejection of such living and *the putting on of a new man* on a level which discards the natural.

The insistence of twice-born religions upon the need for spiritual death on the level of the "natural" plane and rebirth on the higher level of the spiritual has its basis in the fact that the two "lives" cannot coexist in one person: "There are two lives, the natural and the spiritual, and we must lose the one before we can participate in the other."[39] For Christianity and Buddhism, for example, the man "must die to an unreal life before he can be born into the real life."[40]

This division of religions must not be confused with the classification of individual souls into healthy and sick ones. Although there are analogies between such souls and the two types of religions, a fundamental difference must be remembered: the two types of religions never converge, but the contrast between healthy and sick souls may cease to be a radical antagonism in the end. Thus the twice-born Buddha or Loyola and the once-born Emerson, William Ellery Channing, or Theodore Parker may finally all find union with God. Nevertheless, in the history of religion most of the great saints and leaders are to be found among the twice-born souls and in the twice-born religions; *there* are to be found the great forces for developing man's spiritual life in the richest variety of ways and to the greatest dimensions.

VI *Asceticism*

To James, modern Western man has undergone a transformation in his attitudes on the subject of pain; the past expected men to endure or inflict much pain and regarded suffering as an inevitable ingredient of existence, but modern man seeks to avoid and overcome pain. Nevertheless, even in the modern Western world, hardship and suffering still make claims and fill otherwise unrequited essential needs. Even in the comparatively mundane affairs of life the bearing of hardships still is essential; in the religious life the deliberate cultivation of hardships, cheerfully borne, has always been honored: "we see the cultivation of hardship cropping out under every sky and in every faith, as a spontaneous need of character."[41]

This deliberate cultivation of hardship is to be found in connection with every activity that is significant and worthwhile; at its lowest level, it may be simply a revolt against the boredom engendered by ease and comfort; at its highest level, it is an inescapable condition for genuine spiritual growth. Ontologically and religiously, asceticism is associated with "the profounder way of handling the gift of existence."[42] Compared with the ontological seriousness and depths which the *wise* use of asceticism introduces into life, naturalistic optimism is "mere syllabub and flattery and sponge-cake."[43]

On every level of life, a kind of creeping effeminacy threatens to drain out vitality and deeper significance. To fight this effeminacy, unwise men offer completely unacceptable defenses: militarism, imperialism, the assuming of "the white man's burden." While these call for heroism, self-sacrifice, and moral and physical fortitude, they are in themselves so unworthy and degrading that the cure must be seen as worse than the disease.

Twentieth-century man may be forced, therefore, to re-examine the moral and spiritual values attributed to asceticism. He may find in the realm of asceticism desirable *moral equivalents* of war and other undesirable types of the strenuous life: "What we need to discover in the social realm is the moral equivalent of war. . . . I have often thought that in the old monkish poverty-worship . . . there might be something like the moral equivalent of war which we are seeking. May not voluntarily accepted poverty be 'the strenuous life' without the need of crushing weaker peoples?"[44]

Although the strenuous life of the military man and of the man of practical affairs involves self-control and discipline and in that respect resembles the life of an ascetic saint, their lives differ because of the tremendous contrast one finds in all their spiritual concomitants. The heroism and self-severity of the military life are aimed exclusively at destruction and victory; the "asceticism" of the businessman is aimed at the piling up of material wealth. One serves Mars, the other Mammon; in both cases, the soldier and the businessman are nourished by contact with the narrow, non-essential aspects of reality. The religious man, however, who makes *wise* use of ascetical practices, enters into organic relationships with the profoundest dimensions of reality and, in doing so, experiences a tremendous growth of personal powers and freedom.

The aspect of asceticism which appealed most to James was voluntary poverty, and he declared that this freeing of oneself from dependency upon wealth was the most desperate moral need of the contemporary English-speaking world:

Among us English-speaking peoples especially do the praises of poverty need once more to be sung. We have grown literally afraid to be poor. We despise any one who elects to be poor in order to simplify and save his inner life. If he does not join the general scramble and pant with the money-making street, we deem him spiritless and lacking in ambition. We have lost the power even of imagining what the ancient idealization of poverty could have meant: the liberation from material attachments, the unbribed soul, the manlier indifference, the paying our way by what we are or do and not by what we have, the right to fling away our life at any moment irresponsibly,—the more athletic trim, in short, the moral fighting shape. When we of the so-called better classes are scared as men were never scared in history at material ugliness and hardship; when we put off marriage until our house can be artistic, and quake at the thought of having a child without a bank-account and doomed to manual labor, it is time for thinking men to protest against so unmanly and irreligious a state of opinion.

It is true that so far as wealth gives time for ideal ends and exercise to ideal energies, wealth is better than poverty and ought to be chosen. But wealth does this in only a portion of the ideal cases. Elsewhere the desire to gain wealth and the fear to lose it are our chief breeders of cowardice and propagators of corruption. There are thousands of conjunctures in which a wealth-bound man must be a slave, whilst a man for whom poverty has no terrors becomes a freeman. Think of the strength which personal indifference to poverty would give us if we were devoted to unpopular causes. We need no longer hold our tongues or fear to vote the revolutionary or reform ticket. Our stocks might fall, our hopes of promotion vanish, our salaries stop, our club doors close in our faces; yet, while we lived, we would imperturbably bear witness to the spirit, and our example would help to set free our generation. . . .

I recommend this matter to your serious pondering, for it is certain that the prevalent fear of poverty among the educated classes is the worst moral disease from which our civilization suffers.[45]

In assuming the strenuous life of goodness and in striving to overcome the allurements of a life of ease and personal gain, the religious man *hopes* to shift the very center of his being from moral and spiritual trivialities to the fountainhead of all moral and spiritual being. He *wishes* to align himself with the deepest, most creative forces in the universe; he brings into action the profoundest forces of his own being—his moral will power, his faith, and his power of love. He dies to the worldly life of illusions and follies, and by his death he *hopes* to gain true life. His asceticism in the cause of religious faith extinguishes the unworthy tyranny of the flesh and makes possible the freedom of the spirit.

VII *Mysticism*

Although mysticism is generally associated with asceticism, it must *not* be understood as being *produced* by ascetical disciplines. Asceticism is from man; mystical experiences are, to James, gifts of God. The former requires conscious *effort* on the part of man; the latter, *receptivity*. Asceticism operates in the realm of normal consciousness; mysticism transcends this consciousness.

Mystical phenomena held a great fascination for James, for intellectual and personal reasons. Mystical states open up the possibility of other orders of truth distant from those accessible by "ordinary" means. His special interest in cosmic consciousness and panpsychism made mystical eyperiences especially intriguing for him. In addition, there were personal and ancestral reasons why an interest in mysticism should be central in James's religious philosophy. From his father he absorbed a profound spirituality, more perhaps than he was consciously aware of. This heritage, along with his own interest in religion and his empiricism, with its emphasis on original experiences as the source of truth, inevitably made mysticism a fascinating subject.

On the other hand, he insisted that the claims made for mystical experiences must not be accepted uncritically. James's radical empiricism requires that mystical experiences be subjected to the same tests applied to rational beliefs:

> Our own more "rational" beliefs are based on evidence exactly similar in nature to that which mystics quote for theirs. Our senses, namely, have assured us of certain states of fact; but mystical experiences are as direct perceptions of fact for those who have them as any sensations ever were for us. The records show that even though the five senses be in abeyance in them, they are absolutely sensational in their epistemological quality . . .—that is, they are face to face presentations of what seems immediately to exist.[46]

The experiences offered to mankind through mystical phenomena require selection and subordination just as do the experiences which come in the "ordinary," naturalistic world. Possibilities of error and deception occur in dealing with mystical experiences just as they do with the more ordinary ones. But in testing the validity of mystical data, one must not impose upon them the same requirements imposed upon knowledge coming from "rational" sources. To do so would automatically eliminate all mystical experiences from the very start because they are so different from the experiences found in man's normal range of consciousness.

For normal rational beliefs one should insist that they be grounded on "(1) definitely statable abstract principles; (2) definite facts of sensation; (3) definite hypotheses based on such facts; and (4) definite inferences logically drawn."[47] Mystical experiences, by their very nature, are incapable, however, of being articulated in such a manner. It is their nature to be incapable of being handled abstractly or logically.

James proposes that an experience should be called mystical

only when it possesses (1) ineffability, (2) noetic quality, (3) transiency, and (4) passivity.[48] Furthermore, he indicates that "the mystical feeling of enlargement, union, and emancipation has no specific intellectual content whatever of its own."[49] Mysticism contributes to knowledge by greatly enlarging man's field of consciousness, thereby opening up new areas of knowledge and putting "rational" knowledge into truer perspective.

The messages of mystical experiences, though profoundly significant for the one directly involved, have no necessary binding effect on others in the sense that they must accept them uncritically:

> It is evident that from the point of view of their psychological mechanism, the classical mysticism and these lower mysticisms [of delusional insanity] spring from the same mental level, from that great subliminal or transmarginal region. . . . To come from there is no infallible credential. What comes must be sifted and tested, and run the gauntlet of confrontation with the total context of experience, just like what comes from the outer world of sense. Its value must be ascertained by empirical methods, so long as we are not mystics ourselves.[50]

Whatever the non-mystical majority may believe, they should not deny the mystic's right to follow his insights: "If the mystical truth that comes to a man proves to be a force that he can live by, what mandate have we of the majority to order him to live in another way?"[51] The truth of the mystic's beliefs are verified in the same *general way* in which all truths are verified—on the basis of their origination in experience and in terms of the *fruitful* relations which they establish with reality in terms of human conduct. Mystical beliefs, likewise, are also liable to be erroneous just as are beliefs which come from the outer world of sense.

The existence of mystical states, with the knowledge that they furnish, "*absolutely* overthrows the pretensions of the non-mystical states to be the sole and ultimate dictators of what we may believe."[52] The mystical states open up the possibility of other varieties of truth in which, "so far as anything in us vitally responds to them, we may freely continue to have faith."[53]

It is quite possible, or rather most probable, that there are wider and more significant realms of being apart from those which are accessible to man's senses and powers of discursive thought. As a matter of fact, such realms might exceed our world of sense and reason to such an extent as to prove our present "world" but the poorest fragment of reality. To these greater realms, mysticism may have the key. To speak of these greater realms, one must resort to analogies; and James does so on several occasions. He speaks of our human individualities as building accidental fences against the mother-sea or reservoirs of being. He compares man's physical life as lying soaked in a spiritual atmosphere for which men have no present organ of apprehension, just as the lives of domestic pets are set in human environments without being fully conscious of all that exists in such surroundings.

The most significant analogy, however, is "the hypothesis of world-consciousness," which sees the human individual as a fragment, of universal consciousness. This human fragment, artificially isolated from the universal realm of being by the narrowing effects of the senses and reason, gets a certain degree of liberation through the experiences of mystical states. In such states, the individual enjoys contacts in a very limited way with the world-soul or cosmic consciousness. But such contacts, limited though they may be, produce a reorganization of the self of extraordinary depth and range. Some idea of this is obtained also in "normal" states of consciousness when "mystical" data somehow "leak in" from the great sea of cosmic consciousness.

> Just so there is a continuum of cosmic consciousness, against which our individuality builds but accidental fences, and into which our several minds plunge as into a mother-sea or reservoir. Our "normal" consciousness is circumscribed for adaptation to our external earthly environment, but the fence is weak in spots, and fitful influences from beyond leak in, showing the otherwise unverifiable connection. Not only psychic research, but metaphysical philosophy, and speculative biology are led in their own ways to look with favor on some such "panpsychic" view of the universe as this.[54]

In all his discussions of cosmic consciousness and mystical states James attempts to think with a maximum of freedom and often speaks in figures. This fact must be kept in mind as one sees how close his analogies come to affirming a monistic view of reality. Such a viewpoint is completely alien to his philosophy, which is essentially pluralistic in every respect; and monistic figures of speech must not be taken literally in any context. Nevertheless, one must take very seriously his conviction that "rational" consciousness "touches but a portion of the real universe and that our life is fed by the 'mystical' region as well."[55] On this central conviction James speaks with great assurance, especially with reference to knowledge and religion: "If you have intuitions at all, they come from a deeper level of your nature than the loquacious level which rationalism inhabits." "They [mystical states] are states of insight into depths of truth unplumbed by the discursive intellect." "One may say truly, I think, that personal religious experience has its root and centre in mystical states of consciousness. . . ."[56]

VIII *God*

Atheism, deism, and "popular" theism all fail disastrously in expressing the true nature of the divine. Of the three, however, theism, *corrected and purified,* offers the best chance of fruitful knowledge of God.[57] It alone thinks in terms of personality and personal relationships; and, as James declares, personality is, in the world of religion, "the one fundamental fact."[58]

The atheist's arguments against belief in the existence of God belong in the discussion of the problem of faith and knowledge, and there it is seen that such arguments are based ultimately upon the temperamental and subjective preferences of the atheist, just as the *arguments* for God's existence are based finally upon the deep personal preferences of the theist. Thus, from a "purely logical" point of view, theism and atheism are equally admissable; but judged from other points of view—the moral, the spiritual, and the metaphysical—theism is the incomparably superior belief and leads to the better life for man.

Mankind's authentic experiences with the divine, especially man's living in the life of God's love, is so radically different from all other types of experiences, even psychological experiences, that truly religious experiences could not be anticipated in advance of their actual coming. Reason could not suspect their existence because they are "discontinuous with the 'natural' experiences they succeed upon and invert their values."[59] Reason

Philosophy of Religion

cannot anticipate religious experiences, and it is unable by merely rationalistic means to demonstrate the existence of God: "... from the order of the world there is no path to God by coercive reasoning, or even by strong analogy or induction. That we believe in God ... is not due to our logic, but to our emotional wants."[60] That is to say, belief in God is due to faith-creating forces in life which are themselves deeper, broader, and related more intimately to reality than "mere" logic. In other words, God reveals Himself to man in His own ways.

God is revealed especially through man's emotional and volitional needs, which function in a broadly rational sense to establish living connections with the divine. "Our volitional nature must then, until the end of time, exert a constant pressure upon the other departments of the mind to induce them to function to theistic conclusions."[61]

In the human consciousness there is a sense of reality, deeper than the particular "senses" and somehow more authoritative than "pure" reason or logic; there is "*a feeling of objective presence, a perception* of what we may call '*something there*,' more deep and more general than any of the special and particular 'senses' by which current psychology supposes existent reality to be originally revealed."[62]

James's belief in the existence of God is inspired by those very elements of reality which rationalistic thinking most disdains—the particular (as opposed to the general and universal), the personal (as opposed to the coldly impersonal), and the "unwholesome" and the imperfect (as opposed to the "pure" and the perfect). For him, the particulars of existence, the personal data of life, and the very imperfections of reality create a drift of evidence which seems "to sweep us very strongly towards the belief in some forms of superhuman life with which we may, unknown to ourselves, be co-conscious."[63]

> In short, she [pragmatism] widens the search for God. Rationalism sticks to logic and the empyrean. Empiricism sticks to the external senses. Pragmatism is willing to follow either logic or the senses and to count the humblest and most personal experiences. She will count mystical experiences if they have practical consequences. She will take a God who lives in the very dirt of private fact—if that should seem a likely place to find him.[64]

.   .   .   .

Her [pragmatism's] only test of probable truth is what works best in the way of leading us, what fits every part of life best and combines with the collectivity of experience's demands, nothing being omitted. If theological ideas should do this, if the notion of God, in particular, should prove to do it, how could pragmatism possibly deny God's existence?[65]

True knowledge regarding the nature of God is not to be found, therefore, in the pale realm of rationalistic thinking but in the concrete particulars of life. In all of these particulars God is somehow present.

The corrections suggested by James in connection with the theistic views about the nature of God involved a rejection of much of "traditional" theism: "The theological machinery that spoke so lovingly to our ancestors, with its finite age of the world, its creation out of nothing, its juridical morality and eschatology, its relish for rewards and punishments, its treatment of God as an external contriver, and 'intelligent and moral governor,' sounds as odd to most of us as if it were some outlandish savage religion."[66] Many of the cherished tenets of traditional theism were "diseases of the philosophy-shop" that obscured and falsified God's nature and activities and man's relationships with God.

Here again "vicious intellectualism" destroys man's communion with the living God by seeking and establishing abstractions about His nature. As a result, an abstract Absolute is worshipped instead of the living, personal God revealed in authentic religious experiences and described by Pragmatic Empirical religious philosophy: "And the theistic God is almost as sterile a principle [as the Absolute]. You have to go to the world which he has created to get any inkling of his actual character: he is the kind of god that has once for all made that kind of a world. The God of the theistic writers lives on as purely abstract heights as does the Absolute."[67]

God is involved in our individual lives and in our collective histories—His being makes practical differences in our day-to-day existences (and in our external existences, if there be such). He *must* be involved in man's activities if His being is to have the significance required by the pragmatic criterion; as a matter of fact, James requires that God's involvement be so intimate that his views have kinship to "pantheism," seeing God as "the

Philosophy of Religion

indwelling divine rather than external creator, and of human life as part and parcel of that deep reality."[68]

Concern for establishing God as being immanent rather than transcendent led James to speak of his viewpoint as a kind of "pluralistic pantheism." The pantheistic belief that "we are substantially one with it [the deity], and that the divine is therefore the most intimate of all our possessions, heart of our heart," seemed immeasurably superior to the 'older dualistic theism.'"[69] And once it was seen that pantheism need not be confined to the *monistic* form expressed in the philosophy of the Absolute, in which all concrete individuals were swallowed up by the One, James was prepared to approve the other form of pantheism —the *pluralistic* form suggested by radical empiricism:

> ... this pantheistic belief could be held in two forms, a monistic form which I called the philosophy of the absolute, and a pluralistic form which I called radical empiricism, the former conceiving the divine exists authentically only when the world is experienced all at once in its absolute totality, whereas radical empiricism allows that the absolute sum-total of things may never be actually experienced in that shape at all, and that a disseminated, distributed, or incompletely unified appearance is the only form that reality may yet have achieved.[70]

This so-called pluralistic pantheism is not at all a final point of view in itself: it is rather another instrument produced to purify traditional theism from the effects of dualism. In his *purified theism* James expresses his preferred, personal point of view regarding the nature of God. His so-called "pluralistic pantheism" is chiefly, therefore, a device to assert divine immanence against traditional insistence on divine transcendence.

In *Pluralistic Universe* the superiority of James's immanent theism is contrasted with the distortions created by dualistic theism: "This essential dualism of the theistic view has all sorts of collateral consequences. Man being an outsider and a mere subject to God, not his intimate partner, a character of externality invades the field. God is not heart of our heart and reason of our reason, but our magistrate, rather; and mechanically to obey his commands, however strange they may be, remains our only moral duty."[71] Dualistic theism separates God from man, but the purified theism of Pragmatism and Radical Empiricism both restores the union of God and man and respects the personalities of God and man. At the same time, it transforms the universe from a dead mass into a being with whom the *whole* man may have dealings: "At a single stroke, it changes the dead blank *it* of the world into a living *thou,* with whom the whole man may have dealings."[72]

The theism of Pragmatism and Radical Empiricism, in continuing its purification of traditional theism, finds it necessary to reject the doctrine that God is infinite. This doctrine has created false problems in philosophy and religion (such as the problem of evil) and has distorted man's understanding of God and his relations with Him. Pragmatism and Radical Empiricism find no good reasons for asserting that God is infinite, omnipotent, or omniscient. As a matter of fact, very good reasons are found for affirming instead that He is *finite,* although truly the *first among finite beings:*

> Meanwhile the practical needs and experiences of religion seem to me sufficiently met by the belief that beyond each man and in a fashion continuous with him there exists a larger power which is friendly to him and his ideals. All that the facts require is that the power should be both other and larger than our conscious selves. Anything larger will do, if only it be large enough to trust for the next step. It need not be infinite, it need not be solitary. It might conceivably even be only a larger and more godlike self, of which the present self would then be the mutilated expression, and the universe might conceivably be a collection of such selves. . . .[73]

. . . .

> . . . Radical empiricism . . . holding to the each-form, and making of God only one of the eaches, affords the highest degree of intimacy.[74]

. . . .

> First, it is essential that God be conceived as the deepest power in the universe; and, second, he must be conceived under the form of a mental personality. The personality need not be determined intrinsically any further than is involved in the holding of certain things dear, and in the recognition of our dispositions towards those things, the things themselves being all good and righteous things.[75]

. . . .

Philosophy of Religion

"God" in the religious life of ordinary men, is the name not of the whole of things, heaven forbid, but only of the ideal tendency in things, believed in as a super-human person who calls us to co-operate in his purposes, and who furthers ours if they are worthy. He works in an external environment, has limits, and has enemies.[76]

. . . .

Having an environment, being in time, and working out a history, just like ourselves, he escapes the foreignness from all that is human, of the static timeless perfect absolute.[77]

The question of God's existence and problems about His nature must be resolved in terms of the *specific, concrete experiences* which are to be expected as a result of the existence of a being of such a nature: "But all facts are particular facts, and the whole interest of the question of God's existence seems to me to lie in the consequences for particulars which that existence may be expected to entail. That no concrete particular of experience would alter its complexion in consequence of a God being there seems to me an incredible proposition. . . ."[78]

Only on this question may the speculations of dogmatic theology be allowed to stand or fall: Just what are the *concrete consequences* of such and such a doctrine in terms of human experiences? If the answer be "none," or if the consequences be entirely academic, then that doctrine is unworthy of belief, since belief has no significance apart from the conduct to which it leads. Thus judged, the "metaphysical attributes" of God— His aseity and His pure actuality—are unworthy of serious consideration. On the other hand, some of His "moral attributes" are of the greatest significance in the conduct of life:

What shall we say of the attributes called moral? . . . They positively determine fear and hope and expectation, and are foundations for the saintly life. It needs but a glance at them to show how great is their significance.

God's holiness, for example: being holy, God can will nothing but the good . . . Being unalterable, we can count on him securely. These qualities enter into connection with our life, it is highly important that we should be informed concerning them.[79]

On the other hand, to say that "God's essence is to be" is to present a *pragmatically meaningless* statement. It is, in effect, saying nothing at all. But, to say that God is a *personal* being (with whom man can at least hope to have interpersonal communion) is to make a *genuine* affirmation, whether it be true or false. To make a statement about God's nature which leads to good effects in human life is, in turn, to affirm a genuine truth: thus, the affirmation that God is a personal being with whom men may commune (so that God and men "both have purposes for which they care, and each can hear the other's call"[80]) leads to the profoundest improvements in man's conduct and is *verified accordingly in morally good deeds.*

To know truths about God is, therefore, not an intellectualistic process or product; moreover, man's destiny does not consist in enjoying a purely speculative knowledge of God. In harmony with the teachings of Christ, men are said to be saved not by their own *words* but by their God-inspired *deeds.* God is not known by abstract statements, but is revealed truly in man's godlike actions, thoughts and emotions: "To co-operate with his creation by the best and rightest responses seems all he wants of us. In such co-operation with his purposes, not in any chimerical speculative conquest of him, not in any theoretical drinking of him up, must lie the real meaning of our destiny."[81]

Apart from vital responses called for by God's presence, His existence would have no meaning (and therefore no truth) for mankind. A "depersonalized" or non-personal god, being meaningless, would be a falsehood. Thus, for example, the Unknowable of Herbert Spencer could not serve as a substitute for the personal God of theism: "Mere existence commands no reverence whatever, or any emotion, until its quality is specified. Neither does mere cosmic 'power,' unless it make for something which can claim kinship from our sympathies. . . . As well might you speak of being irreverent to Space or disrespectful to the Equator."[82]

God's reality is made known to man not in general abstractions but in specific acts of love, in concrete claims made upon man, and in the loving assistance which God provides for the fulfillment of His claims: "But the only force of appeal to *us*, which either a living God or an abstract ideal order can wield, is found in the 'everlasting ruby vaults' of our own human

Philosophy of Religion

hearts, as they happen to beat responsive and not irresponsive to the claim. So far as they do feel it when made by a living consciousness, it is life answering to life. A claim thus livingly acknowledged is acknowledged with a solidity and a fullness which no thought of an 'ideal' backing can render complete. . . ."[83]

The belief that "God exists," when translated into its pragmatic meaning, says that the permanent preservation of an ideal order is guaranteed and that where God is, "tragedy is only provisional and partial, and shipwreck and dissolution [are] not the absolutely final things."[84] In affirming belief in God's existence, most religious men are testifying to their conviction "that not only they themselves, but the whole universe of beings to whom God is present, are secure in His parental hands. . . . God's existence is the guarantee of an ideal order that shall be permanently preserved."[85]

IX Man's Images of God

The validity of man's beliefs about God is to be determined, like the validity of all other kinds of knowledge, by the practical, concrete consequences which particular beliefs have in human life.

For most men it is "necessary" to conceive of God as a personal being, and this image is abundantly verified by its fruits in human experiences. Man's spiritual life and the hardships of the moral order call for help and guidance, which only a divine thinker and co-worker can provide. The human desire, for example, for a "stable and systematic moral universe" is fully possible only in a world "where there is a divine thinker with all-enveloping demands."[86] In addition, the religious view not only incites man's strenuous moral activities but also takes "our joyous, careless, trustful moments, and it justifies them."[87]

James believes that many of the older images of God as an external judge, as the Great Architect, as a majestic king, were useful and appropriate in the ages which originated them. But, having advanced morally and intellectually to a point where these concepts becloud the improved images of God available at this stage of history, man must work vigorously to free himself from their influences and to develop concepts that are more worthy of God and more fruitful in human lives. For example,

God must not be pictured as a "gentleman" but rather as a co-worker with man, fitted for menial services; man is not to be conceived as God's valet, but rather God and men are to be understood as collaborators in the vast task of building a moral universe. In this task much menial work must be done, and God does not assign His share to deputies. In this image, God is not above "dirtying His own hands" with the works of creation or of redemption: "The prince of darkness may be a gentleman, as we are told he is, but whatever the God of earth and heaven is, he can surely be no gentleman. His menial services are needed in the dust of our human trails, even more than his dignity is needed in the empyrean."[88]

X God and the Saints

A man is a saint when the "spiritual emotions are the habitual centre of the personal energy"; "the collective name for the ripe fruits of religion in a character is Saintliness."[89] Saintliness, its lofty character notwithstanding, must also be subjected to the pragmatic test; the fruits of character determine the genuineness of holy lives: "What I then propose to do is, briefly stated, to test saintliness by common sense, to use human standards to help us decide how far the religious life commends itself as an ideal kind of human activity. If it commends itself, then, any theological beliefs that may inspire it, in so far forth will stand accredited. If not, then they will be discredited, and all without reference to anything but human working principles."[90]

The usefulness of saints has been denied and Christian morality described as the morality of slaves. Against the "pseudo-virtues" of the meek Christian, with his pity for the weak and wretched, the militant virtues of the strong man have been extolled as begettors of genuine progress. Against the attacks of the "strong man" can the claims of saintly merits be maintained?

> The whole feud [between the ideals of the saint and those of the "strong man"] revolves essentially on two pivots: Shall the seen world or the unseen world be our chief spheres of adaptation? and must our means of adaptation in this seen world be agressiveness or non-resistance?

> The debate is serious. In some sense and to some degree both worlds must be acknowledged and taken account of; and in the seen world both aggressiveness and non-resistance are needful. It is a question of emphasis, more or less. Is the saint's type or the strong-man's type the more ideal?[91]

Measured in terms of the development of an ideal human society, the Nietzschean strong man's type of humanity is inferior to that of the saint's. A society of saints would be immeasurably superior to a society created by a Nietzschean strong man; in the former, there would be no aggressiveness, but only sympathy and fairness. "Abstractly considered, such a society on a large scale would be the millennium, for every good thing might be realized there with no expense of friction. To such a millennial society the saint would be entirely adapted. . . . The saint is therefore abstractly a higher type of man than the 'strong man,' because he is adapted to the highest society conceivable, whether that society ever be concretely possible or not."[92]

The special role of saints is to be the "authors, auctores, increasers of goodness." Their greatest contribution is to be found in the human charity "which we find in all saints, and great excess of it which we find in some saints." This charity is a "genuinely creative social force, tending to make real a degree of virtue which it alone is ready to assume as possible."[93] In social evolution, this charity is vital and essential.

Through the saints, God's collaboration with mankind reaches its greatest effectiveness. His inspiration and power flood the saint, who, patiently, passively, waits on the divine will. The unseen world, with which the saint seeks to conform his life, provides beatific bliss, which at the same time most often also brings the power to make extensive, practical changes in the world. The genuineness of the saint's holy bliss is witnessed to by the ways in which his life transforms this world.

In the final analysis, the holy man's greatest and most practical contribution to mankind is his own remarkable life. Thus Christ's greatest gift to man is—Christ; and the religion of Jesus is Jesus.

CHAPTER 7

The Universe

JAMES'S ATTITUDES toward the universe were profoundly reverential; but his reverence was directed toward the temporal rather than the eternal, the many rather than the few. His temperament and his philosophy revealed a preference for the authentic individual with its multitudinous associations rather than the abstractly isolated individual; for the dynamic rather than the static; for the concrete and particular rather than the abstract and universal; and for the open, unfinished universe rather than a closed, completed one.

He preferred to assume that man's presence in the universe means that man is truly a *part*—a *significant* part—of the universe; he believed that the truest philosophical and scientific accounts of reality must take into consideration man's dynamic *participation* in the workings and destiny of the world and must include the roles of the volitional and emotional aspects of human nature. So-called "objective" theories of reality that left out such essential human dimensions, he believed, were hopelessly false.

Much of philosophy, by means of determinism, intellectualism, and absolutism, falsifies reality and makes man an alien in the world. What is needed is a philosophy that will restore to man the living unity of his experience. Such a philosophy will not be overawed by the mechanical side of reality; it will not falsely overemphasize the theoretical and rationalistic aspects of knowledge; it will, on the other hand, "break up this cast-iron monistic . . . vision, and substitute for it an open universe, giving place to novelty that would allow for ethical strivings on the basis of free will.[1]"

The Universe

I Monism

For those who prize logic, consistency, regular pattern and predictability and who are charmed by perfection and completeness, the monistic account of reality is most appealing. This appeal has given rise to the great monistic systems, notably Hegel's Absolute Idealism and Spencer's Systematic Philosophy, both involving the "block-universe," which stands as the antithesis of James's world view:

> For this monism [Absolute Idealism] the essence of rationality consists in conceiving the universe as a rigid logical system, (or in James's phrase) as a "block-universe," in which every part is determined through-and-through by its relation to the whole. In such a system the distinction between past, present, and future is avowedly illusory, and altogether irrelevant to the central core of reality. So far as mundane events are allowed to have reality—and *how* far they have any is treated as a trivial and almost frivolous question, on which serious philosophy is under no obligation to make up its mind—future events are just as real, and just as fixed as the whole past. *So far* as the historical process is real, it is the "progressive revelation" or "manifestation" (illuminating phrase!) of what in its essential "logical" nature is a perfect and timeless Whole.[2]

James's espousal of "humanism" as against monism is a response to *a multiplicity of truths* long denied or ignored by "vicious" intellectualism. By affirming humanistic truths, James hopes to liberate the human spirit from the distortions of rationalism.

> And, finally, he [the reader] should ask himself why a doctrine which maintains, as Humanism maintains against Absolutism, that human ideals must really count in the making of reality, is regarded as low and spiritually degrading. Is it not, rather, clear that Humanism, by questioning the absolutist notion of "truth," and breaking down the distinction between "theory" and "practice," vindicates the reality of that whole world of life and action which Absolutism had contemptuously dismissed as "mere appearance"? Which is in truth the nobler destiny—to take an active part in the real shaping of an as yet unfinished future, or to contemplate, at an infinite distance, the Absolute's beatific vision of bogus existence in hallucinatory time?[3]

Whatever man's views of the universe may be, therefore, they should include room for human emotions, moral freedom, and responsibility. Monism, whether the evolutionary monism of Spencer or the idealistic monism of Hegel, leaves no room for the full human person and contradicts those experiences which testify to the existence of real novelties and changes.

In 1903, James enumerated his objections to monism in unpublished rough notes for his "Seminary in Metaphysics, 1903-4":

1) Doesn't account well for finite consciousness. (Represents us as characters in a novel, but they don't walk off—Absolute knows us *cum alio*, we know ourselves *sine alio*. With our experience goes pain. My griefs at least are mine.)
2) Introduces problem of evil. If Perfection came first, why any imperfection? (Lotze on Leibnitz, etc.)
3) Its eternal would contradict character and expression of reality. Novelty, achievement, gain!
4) Fatalistic. Violates free will. Makes notion of possible illusory. Pluralism the *moralistic* view. Perfection necessary versus perfection conditionally possible.

Would you accept the latter world? Of course![4]

The unity of the universe is not that of absolute oneness. The unity which it has is one made up of the external relations between discrete "things" and the unity which is made by man, particularly by his thinking about things. ("World is many in all respects except that its parts can be thought together."[5])

The most effective objections to monism are logical and ethical ones. Ethically, one objects to the belief that vicious crimes are a necessary part of the universe; and, logically, one becomes lost in trying to understand how absolute perfection gives rise to imperfections: "It [monism] creates a problem of evil. Evil, for pluralism, presents only the practical problem of how to get rid of it. For monism the problem is theoretical: How—if Perfection be the source, should there be Imperfection? If the world as known to the Absolute be perfect, why should it be known otherwise, in myriads of inferior editions also? The perfect edition surely was enough. How do the breakage and dispersion and ignorance get in?"[6]

II *Pluralism*

Experience reveals neither absolute oneness nor absolute manyness, but a mixture of unity and manyness. Neither seems to be the more essential; and, if the misshaping activities of vicious intellectualism are avoided, it becomes clear that they are "co-ordinate features of the natural world."[7] Following the pattern of daily experience, pluralists say that the universe is *loosely connected*, having connections that are real without being such as to determine *completely* the activities of "things." Nothing shows better the dissolving effect of false intellectualism than the annihilation of the real conjunctions found in experience and the consequent need to invent an idealistic basis for connections and interactions.

> But the purely verbal character of the operation is undisguised. Because the *names* of finite things and their relations are disjoined, it doesn't follow that the realities named need a *deus ex machina* from on high to conjoin them. The same things disjoined in one respect *appear* as conjoined in another. Naming the disjunction doesn't debar us from also naming the conjunction in a later modifying statement, for the two are absolutely co-ordinate elements in the finite tissue of experience.[8]

This recognition, as previously noted, of real connections in being distinguishes James's Radical Empiricism from that of his British predecessors Hume and Mill, both of whom "succumbed to that atomistic associationism which was empiricism's fatal malady."[9] James declared that the *connections* between things, being given in experience *along* with things, are just as real as anything else given in experience. In an unpublished note, he spoke of his "philosophy of *pluralism with continuity*." He declared: "The monists posit chasms a priori and then negate or overcome them by the higher unities which they invoke"; whereas he believes that continuity is an original feature of the universe, "since no break or chasm is to be found."[10]

James's *radically empirical* approach to reality makes his pluralistic treatment fair to both the elements of distinctiveness and of relationship found in experience. Although he thunders against the greatest of superstitions, "the idolatry of the *Whole*,"[11] he denies any suggestion that the "eaches" which make up the universe have no connections with one another: ". . . pluralism itself is a noun of unity. A 'many' as such is already unified":[12]

> If the each-form be the eternal form of reality no less than it is the form of temporal appearance, we still have a coherent world, and not an incarnate incoherence, as is charged by so many absolutists. Our "multiverse" still makes a "universe"; for every part, tho it not be in actual or immediate connexion, is nevertheless in some possible or mediated connexion, with every other part however remote, through the fact that each part hangs together with its very next neighbors in inextricable confusion. . . . It is what I call the strung-along type, the type of continuity, contiguity, or concatenation.[13]

The pluralist energetically strives to avoid the abstractions of both the absolute idealists and the materialists, who, in the interests of some favored features of reality, systematically eliminate all other features. Materialism, preferring to explain the "higher" aspects of being by the "lower," gives "the lower elements the foremost place in being and power."[14] Idealism, on the other hand, denigrates the concrete, material, and temporal in the "interests" of the spiritual. In both cases vicious intellectualism is at work, distorting reality with the deadly misuse of abstraction.

Pluralism objects to this intellectualistic imperialism and affirms the philosopher's obligation to approach all types of being in an unbiased manner. James presents the analogy of a fellowship of citizens as a way of describing the relationships among various types of beings:

> Why may not the world be a sort of republican banquet of this sort, where all the qualities of being respect one another's personal sacredness, yet sit at the common table of space and time?
> To me this view seems deeply probable. Things cohere, but the act of cohesion itself implies but few conditions, and leaves the rest of their qualifications undeterminate.[15]

In this fellowship of beings are found values as well as other existences; moral free will as well as scientific regularities; the human emotions as well as the human intellect. They are bound together, freely, in a unity that is not absolute or external but

The Universe

united in "the principle of *experienced continuity*," which is "the general unifier of the world."¹⁶

This *pluralism* with *unity* not only characterizes the metaphysical aspects of being but also characterizes "the practically real world for each one of us." There, various physical facts and emotional values which make up "the effective world of the individual" combine indistinguishably. If either factor, physical or emotional, be withdrawn or perverted, the result would be "the kind of experience we call pathological."¹⁷

Pluralism, generally speaking, is a revolt against absolutism and an assertion of moral and religious values. "It agrees with the moral and dramatic expressiveness of life."¹⁸

> Singulars! Description can't exhaust them.
> They lead, as concepts don't lead, to ejective
>   present reality.
> In what sense? If pragmatism be true
>   how can we admit ejects which
>   are never matters for experience?
> Concepts hitherwood and concepts thitherwood
>   of perception.
> Simplest case: your body continuous as
>   natural object.
> Other case: objects connected with both our
>   bodies. Coterminous.¹⁹

III *Tychism*

Real *growth*, involving new events and new beings, is an essential part of James's universe. Considering the reality or unreality of *novelty* as the final pragmatic difference between monism and pluralism, James says that the proponents of pluralism defend the position that mankind may be the author of genuine novelties. That genuine novelties can come into being is inconceivable in the closed, completely determined universe of the monists; but the pragmatic world made up of loosely connected beings is a world in which novelty, chance, and growth play essential parts. This belief James calls "tychism."

Monists, determined to explain reality *conceptually*, rationalize the world in such a way that novelty could not possibly be admitted. From the viewpoint of conception, the so-called principle of causality, for example, requires that the effect somehow already exist in the cause and that the effect be not absolutely novel but similar to the cause. Moreover, the very process of conceptualization involves the elimination of change and process, the substitution of static concepts for dynamic perceptions, so that the changes which are essential parts of experience are abstracted away.

James, insisting that Intellectualism butchers reality, declares that the process of change is a fundamental fact of human experience. He suggests that "the concrete perceptual flux, taken just as it comes, offers in our own activity-situations perfectly comprehensible instances of causal agency,"[20] and does so in such a way as to show that genuine novelty is compatible with the principle of causality. "Here [in the concrete movements of our soul] is our deepest organ of communication with the nature of things. . . . For here possibilities, not finished facts, are the realities with which we have actively to deal."[21]

The question as to whether there be real novelties in the universe (with the possibility of real *choices* by man) cannot be settled conclusively by intellectualistic "proofs." "What divides us into possibility men and anti-possibility men is different faiths or postulates,—postulates of rationality. To this man the world seems more rational with possibilities in it,—to that man more rational with possibilities excluded; and talk as we will about having to yield to evidence, what makes us monists or pluralists, determinists or indeterminists, is at bottom always some sentiment like this."[22]

It is perfectly possible that in the flux of sensible experience itself there is a rationality which has been overlooked by philosophers. In this rationality, rather than in that of the static realm of concepts, may be found the facts about novelty, change, and process. The philosopher, therefore, must intelligently study sensible experience; there in the continuously developing experiential series he will find *concrete perceptions* of novelty and causality. On reflection, he will discover a moral coherence which is fully as rational as the logical coherence of intellectualism. He will discover there a genuine alternative to the monistic determinism which, making all the crimes and sins of history inevitable, violates man's sense of morality through and through.

"We cannot explain conceptually *how* genuine novelty can come; but if one did come we could experience that it came.

The Universe

We do, in fact, experience novelties all the while. Our perceptual experience overlaps our conceptual reason: the *that* transcends the *why*."[23] Novelty, as man experiences it, does not need to appear abruptly; and James, as he developed his views, came to believe that the novel, while inexplicable, might develop gradually and somehow belong to the context in which it arose.[24] "Novelty," he said, "as empirically found, doesn't arrive by jumps and jolts, it leaks in insensibly, for adjacents in experience are always interfused. . . ."[25]

In 1902, in an outstanding bit of rigorous reasoning, the arguments for tychism were summed up by James:

Reasons in Tychism's favor.

i Scientific reasons:
1. No concrete experience ever repeats itself. The usual explanation of concrete variety by permutation of unvarying elements, is, if taken absolutely, only an assumption. Scientific laws express only aggregate results, compatible with individual variation in the elements—recent science abounds in the admission of such variation.
2. We fail to absolutely exclude originality, by assuming that elements only *repeat*. Repeat what? Original models!
3. Our own decisions suggest what "coming into existence" might be like: "Chance" from without, self-sufficing life from within. *What* comes is determined only *when* it comes. *Ab extra* it appears only as a possible gift or "graft."

ii Moral reasons:
1. Absolutely to deny novelty, as Monism does, and to assume that the universe has exhausted its spontaneity in one act, shocks our sense of life.
2. Tychism, essentially pluralistic, goes with empiricism, personalism, democracy, and freedom. It believes that unity is in process of being genuinely won. In morals it bases obligation on actual demand. Tychism and "external relations" stand or fall together. They mean genuine individuality, something sacred from without, *taboo*.

iii Metaphysical reasons:
1. Tychism eliminates the "problem of evil" from theology.
2. It has affinities with common-sense in representing the Divine as finite.
3. It avoids Monism's doubling-up of the world into two editions, the Finite repeating the Absolute in inferior form.[26]

IV *The Open Universe*

The doctrine of the open universe follows as a development of the belief that novelty and chance are to be found in reality. Believing that "things may arise plurally by chance (tychism')," [27] James says that *things form a universe after they have arisen.* "The essence of my contention," he declares, "is that in a world where connections are not logically necessary they may nevertheless adventitiously 'come.' Series of independent origin and purpose may inosculate by 'chance-encounter,' and therefore mingle their causalties and combine their effects." [28] It is possible that the world may very well be fluid and growing, rather than absolutely fixed and finished.

To James, it seems most likely that the universe is discontinuous to some extent and pluralistic, without, however, being so pluralistic as to make unlikely a fruitful outcome of our human venture: "It overflows, exceeds, and alters. It may turn into novelties, and can be known adequately only by following its singularities from moment to moment as our experience grows. Empiricist philosophy thus renounces the pretension to an all-inclusive vision." [29]

Three years before his death, James, in writing to Henri Bergson, modestly expressed his dissatisfaction with his own explanation of the open universe. He told Bergson that *he* had "set things straight at a single stroke by your fundamental conception of the continuously creative nature of reality." [30] He declared that he and Bergson were both fighting for tychism and "a really growing world." [31]

V *A Melioristic Universe*

In defending the concept of an open universe, James is carefully constructing a world in which man's experience of moral freedom will be validated and in which human actions may play significant parts. He feels that it is entirely right for human beings to desire intimate relations with the universe and to wish them to be satisfactory ones. But nature in the raw has no features which of themselves command man's respect. Nature herself appears, *en grosse,* to be indifferent to human values: "Visible nature is all plasticity and indifference—a moral multi-

The Universe

verse . . . and not a moral universe. To such a harlot we owe no allegiance."[32]

But this viewpoint in which nature is regarded unselectively as a mass of experiences speaks with no special authority and cannot be maintained for any length of time. Some sort of selection is forced upon man, both in unphilosophic activities, such as finding food and shelter and in the organization of sciences and philosophies. Whatever principle of selection is employed will determine much about the nature of the resulting "universe," and in this sense all worlds will be anthropomorphic. Thus the "rigorously impersonal view of science"—being just one of the many possible ways of proceeding in the construction of a universe—may very well "one day appear as having been a temporarily useful eccentricity rather than the definitively triumphant position which the sectarian scientist at present so confidently announces it to be."[33]

In selecting from the endless stream of experience data to make a universe, the intellectualistic tendency to give *abstraction* supreme, irresponsible authority produces worlds which are basically most irrational because they fail to satisfy the mind's desire for a rational universe. Thus the materialistic point of view, in reducing or eliminating all spiritual data develops a world which denies man's very rational desire for a universe invested with genuine significance.

Seeing himself in nature and seeing his beliefs and aspirations as part of the universe of realities, man legitimately keeps with him these beliefs and aspirations as he forms his views and shapes his world. As a matter of fact, he *must* do so, be he monist or pluralist, theist or atheist. He will see in nature what he believes should be there, because it *is* there either concretely or as a result of his own abstractions: "The outward face of nature need not alter, but the expressions of meaning in it alters. It is dead and is alive again. It is like the difference between looking on a person without love, or upon the same person with love. In the latter case intercourse springs into new vitality. So when one's affections keep in touch with the divinity of the world's authorship, fear and egotism fall away. . . ."[34]

The open universe, by reason of its incompleteness and loosely connected parts, offers the possibility of an ideal order, not as an origin but as an ultimate towards which the world, with man's cooperation, may move. In such a universe, the ideal order will be an *extract* from the whole rather than the whole itself. The pragmatist believes that some of "the conditions of the world's salvation are actually extent" and that, "should the residual conditions come[,] salvation would be an accomplished reality."[35]

While man is in one sense a passive portion of the universe, in another sense he shows "a curious autonomy, as if we were small active centres on our own account."[36] Thus man's faith may be regarded as a formative factor in the universe, and men must be seen as "co-determinants, by our behavior, of what its total character may be."[37] Man's acts, to some extent, determine the nature of the world.

To the extent that the future of the universe is created by the actions of its parts, its "success" depends upon the ways in which various parts work for their ideals. For man this incomplete, imperfect world is well suited in the sense that it, far more so than a "perfect" universe, offers him a challenge and an opportunity for growth and sacrifice. This imperfect universe is morally suited to mankind: "Will not every one instantly declare a world fitted only for fair-weather human beings susceptible of every passive enjoyment, but without independence, courage, or fortitude, to be from a moral point of view incommensurably inferior to a world framed to elicit from man the every form of triumphant endurance and conquering moral energy."[38]

Of course, even though one man or all men should do *their* best, it does not necessarily follow that other parts of the universe will do likewise; and so good will and labor could be negated. Nevertheless, it is best for one to proceed with his good works since he *must* take one of four attitudes regarding the cooperation of other active powers: "(1) Follow intellectualist advice: wait for evidence; and while waiting, do nothing; or (2) *Mistrust* the other powers and, sure that the universe will fail, *let* it fail; or (3) Trust them; and at any rate do *our* best, in spite of the *if;* or, finally, *Flounder,* spending one day in one attitude, another day in another."[39]

The third attitude appears to be the only wise way, and so a man should proceed with his good works.

The Universe

"If we do *our* best, *and* the other powers do *their* best, the world will be perfected"—this proposition expresses no actual fact, but only the complexion of a fact thought of as eventually possible. As it stands, *no* conclusion can be positively deduced from it. . . .

We can *create* the conclusion, then. We can and we may, as it were, jump with both feet off the ground into or towards a world of which we trust the other parts to meet our jump—and *only so* can the *making* of the perfected world of the pluralistic pattern ever take place. Only through our precursive trust in it can it come into being.[40]

CHAPTER *8*

The Moral Life of Man

JAMES'S PHILOSOPHY begins and ends with the insistence that in this life men must be able to fulfill their moral aspirations. Every phase of his thinking is oriented around the problem of good and evil and man's elemental need to lead a life of moral significance. Pragmatism, Radical Empiricism, the open universe, a finite, paternal God, indeterminism, and tychism, collectively describe, therefore, a world in which man may work out a moral destiny. The radical question of life—whether at bottom this universe is moral or amoral—must be answered with a thundering affirmative: "Is the world a simple brute actuality, an existence *de facto* about which the deepest thing that can be said is that it happens so to be; or is the judgment of *better* or *worse*, of ought, as intimately pertinent to phenomena as the simple judgment *is* or *is not?*"[1]

Man's deepest experiences lead him to believe that good and evil are objectively real; that the universe is both breeding ground and battleground of good and evil; that human participation is essential in the moral struggle; and that by his participation man's own fate is determined. For man, life "feels *like* a real fight—as if there were something really wild in the universe which we, with our idealities and faithfulness, are needed to redeem."[2]

This universe, with its evils to be endured and overcome by human valor, thrilled James. He loved its hawk-like flavor; he preferred it infinitely to the insipid, characterless "goodness" of the respectable people at the Chautauqua, where he yearned for the sudden sound of a pistol shot or for an elopement to break the monotony of deadly respectability. In his love for the good fight aimed at destroying deadly moral evils, he resembled "our Heracles," as described vividly by Epictetus:

The Moral Life of Man

> Or what do you think Heracles would have amounted to, if there had not been a lion like the one which he encountered, and a hydra, and a stag, and a boar, and wicked and brutal men, whom he made it his business to drive out and clear away? And what would he have been doing had nothing of the sort existed? Is it not clear that he would have rolled himself up in a blanket and slept? In the first place, then, he would never have become Heracles by slumbering away his whole life in such luxury and ease; but even if he had, what good would he have been? What would have been the use of those arms of his and of his prowess in general, and his steadfastness and nobility, had not such circumstances and occasions roused and excited him? What then? Ought he to have prepared these for himself and sought to bring a lion into his own country from somewhere or other, and a boar and a hydra? This would have been a folly and madness. But since they did exist and were found in the world, they were servicable and a means of revealing and exercising our Heracles.[3]

The lion, the hydra, the stag, the boar, and the wicked men, thus viewed, make possible the development of the heroism of Heracles. And the world, with all its evils, seems to exist for the greatest enrichment of human consciousness and for the maximum development of man's moral life.

I *Legalistic Morality*

To Decalogue-oriented, cult-oriented, or civil law-oriented good persons, the essence of morality consists in *obeying objective rules* without variation in all kinds of situations. Excessive, and sometimes pre-emptive, emphasis upon *proscription*, however, distorts the nature of the moral life, which always calls for *more* than merely obeying commandments; sometimes, indeed, morality involves acting *against* the letter or spirit of accepted rules.

Too often, society substitutes indoctrination in prescribed forms of thought and action in the place of genuine moral education. In the process, not only is genuine morality bypassed, but the installation of a substitute makes its emergence practically impossible. Philistine ethics and the pseudo-morality of narrow interests become installed; and, with all their rigidities, they are only remotely responsive to the moral facts of life.

Genuine morality will avoid abstract and remote ways of

considering individual facts; it will never completely divorce its generalizations from the human situations from which they arose and to which they refer. If this morality be *theistic*, it will refer constantly to God as a person and not merely adhere to His commandments, seeing that God is working for man's salvation not only in making rules but also in an endless variety of encounters with mankind. If a genuine morality be *humanistic*, it also will keep its abstract and general rules subordinated to the total human personality, which has claims and demands that cannot be completely expressed in rules. In both instances, it will be maintained that rules do not in themselves carry the full riches of the moral life.

The unfathomable potentialities of development in human souls call for a wisdom that cannot be adequately embodied in legislation. Thinking that souls are adequately provided for when rules have been created and proclaimed is at best an arrant example of abstractionism. The abstractionist, legislating for souls, ignores the tremendous diversities of character in various persons and speaks as if there were "one intrinsically ideal type of human character" to which his rules must be applied uniformly. The empiricist, however, respecting the diversity of characters, sees that there is no intrinsically ideal type of character; and he declares that moralists must take this diversity into account when providing moral guidance: "No two of us have identical difficulties, nor should we be expected to work out identical solutions. Each, from his peculiar angle of observation, takes in a certain sphere of fact and trouble, which each must deal with in a unique manner. One of us must soften himself, another must harden himself; one must yield a point, another must stand firm,—in order the better to defend the position assigned him."[4]

The highest reaches of morality, with its respect for individuality and its distrust for the narrowly legal and literal virtues, must not, however, be thought of as the subject of arbitrary "originality." Not in ethics, any more than in physics, should one strike out independently and aim at originality. The realm of ethics also has its necessities; the empiricist, in insisting that most moral codes do not accurately or adequately convey the essentials of the moral life, does not endorse antinomianism.

II The Necessary Character of Morality

Moral goodness and evil are introduced into this world by the thoughts and actions of intelligent beings; in the absence of such beings, the universe would be amoral. But this does not mean that *goodness* and *evil per se* are arbitrary products of man—or of God. The moral order rests on an absolute and ultimate "should," which can be appreciated only in connection with James's theory of necessary ideas.

Moral categories and moral imperatives do not arise from extra-experiential sources, such as a World of Forms, and do not depend for their validity upon extra-experiential authority. Looking for external guarantees is one of the greatest follies of non-experiential philosophies: the "guarantee," if there be any, must be *within* the fabric of experience; and James's *radically* experiential philosophy finds it there.

In examining man's aesthetic, intellectual, and moral experiences, concepts are found which cannot be explained as the products of "ordinary" experience; and James, as previously indicated, in *The Principles of Psychology*, is led to describe two types of experience: the "ordinary" or "front-door" type, which enters through the senses and which immediately becomes the mind's object; and the "house-born" or "back-door" experiences which originate "inside" the person. The agents of such back-door experiences are in the brain itself or elsewhere in the body, being natural objects or processes "which equally modify the brain, but mould it to no cognition of *themselves*."[5]

Human ideals do not originate in sensory experiences; such ideals *are often in conflict with experiences originating in the senses*. In the moral realm, house-born ideals often war with front-door experiences. As James points out, "the early Christian with his kingdom of heaven" tells the world "that the existing order must perish, root and branch, ere the true order can come."[6]

Although ethics may, therefore, never establish complete congruence between its ideals and the order of time-and-space relations, still it is possible to develop a "system" of ethics in which ethical data are conceptualized to provide a guide for future conduct. As a matter of fact, such a system, if based on *the necessary character of moral judgments,* may become a genuine science of morality.

In ethics, as in aesthetics, man invincibly craves to alter the given order of experience. Certain types of conduct, he feels, should not be so, just as certain colors or compositions ought to be otherwise. Why does man thus feel dissatisfied with moral and aesthetic experiences? He feels so because he is affected by standards of moral and aesthetic excellence by which concrete experiences are judged as invariably unsatisfactory, to some extent.

Whence these standards? Certainly they do not arise from the imperfect data of external experiences. Nor can they be explained as arising from habit, or usualness, or the inherited experiences of the race; for a man's standards often involve disapproval of the habitual, the usual, and the biological, or the cultural traditions of his race or community. The necessity found in moral (and aesthetic) standards cannot have been engendered by external experiences; as a matter of fact, the exact opposite is true. The necessity, instead of being engendered by the external experiences, is what actually engenders the experiences.

In the absence of moral imperatives of a necessary character, actions would have no moral significance at all. Man would see neither good nor evil in them nor any imperative regarding them if he did not already know that good and evil are *real* and are *necessarily* opposed. In this sense the inner relations of the ideas of good and evil and obligation "engender" the external experiences. These *"ideal and inward relations amongst the objects of our thought . . . can in no intelligible sense whatever be interpreted as reproductions of the order of outer experience."*[7] And expressing the same thought positively, James says, "There is no denying the fact that *the mind is filled with necessary and eternal relations which it finds between certain of its ideal conceptions, and which form a determinate system, independent of the order of frequency in which experience may have associated the conception's originals* in time and space."[8]

Thus, for example, the concept of justice has its necessary features. To be *justice* it must mean exactly what *justice* means; it must not be the self-interest of the stronger party, "might makes right," posing as "justice." To say that it is "might disguised" is simply to create another question: if might is disguised

The Moral Life of Man

as justice, *what is justice?* Certainly, it is something essentially different from might, and no amount of verbal juggling will make *justice* anything but *justice*. If it is to exist at all, in the realm of concepts or in the world of space-and-time relations, justice is necessarily one thing and nothing else; and the just man will be always aware of the lack of justice in numberless situations in the world.

The necessity found in moral concepts such as justice is analogous to that found in concepts in other realms, such as those of color:

> Take blueness and yellowness, for example. We can operate on them in some ways, but not in other ways. We can compare them, but we cannot add one to or substract it from the other. We can refer them to a common kind, color; but we cannot make one a kind of the other, or infer one from the other. This has nothing to do with [external] experience. For we *can* add blue *pigment* to yellow *pigment*, and substract it again, and get a result both times. Only we know perfectly that this is no addition or subtraction of the blue and yellow qualities or natures themselves.[9]

Therefore, *if* there are to be ethical concepts at all, they will have some necessary characteristics. That there *are* ethical concepts and that they *must be obeyed* are facts disclosed to man in the fabric of his experience.

III *Objective Ethics*

Although the Empiricist denies the existence of any abstract moral "nature of things" and thereby eliminates the possibility of any set of moral ideals existing apart from specific, morally responsible beings, he does not mean to imply that moral standards do not exist. Neither does he intend to say that morality is a private, subjective matter in which individual whims or selfish interests may be received as a valid standard for conduct.

On the contrary, James believes that there is an *absolute* morality found in the lives of men that has in turn its analogue in the universe, which displays a "seriousness" paralleling the nobility of human morality. The basis for this absolute morality is found entirely within the context of man's experience, requiring no *a priori* or trans-empirical references. Its objective standards grow up endogenously *within* human lives.

In discussing ethics, the moral philosopher should distinguish between the psychological, the metaphysical, and the casuistic questions and discuss them separately. The psychological question has to do with the historical origin of man's moral ideals; the metaphysical investigates the meaning of *good, evil,* and *obligation;* and the casuistic question "asks what is the *measure* of the various goods and ills which men recognize, so that the philosopher may settle the true order of human obligations."[10]

Moral ideas, as has been seen already, originate as "house-born" experiences, the products of purely inward forces. They cannot be explained as products of the evolution of the species; as a matter of fact, *the more penetrating ideals are revolutionary,* presenting themselves "far less in the guise of effects of past experience than in that of probable causes of future experience, factors to which the environment and the lessons it has so far taught us must learn to bend."[11] For example, the ideals of the first Abolitionists, in their moral war against slavery, speak less of the effects of the past than of the future in which the environment will be modified by new freedom.

IV *The Person and Morality*

Moral ideals, of course, cannot be discussed apart from the words *goodness, badness,* and *obligation.* These in turn can exist only when they have been realized by some sentient being. Such a being, so far as he feels anything to be good, makes it good; and, if he were the only sentient being, its being good for him would make it absolutely good, "for he is the sole creator of values in that universe, and outside of his opinion things have no moral character at all."[12] In such a moral solitude, there would be no moral standard for judging the rightness or wrongness of his opinions because "beyond the facts of his own subjectivity there is nothing moral in the world."[13]

When several sentient beings co-exist, it is probable that they would not agree on moral judgments, and then the world would lack ethical unity. The only alternatives here are to accept the implicit universal subjectivism (which is unacceptable to James) or to find some casuistic scale. The ranking of ideals must not be achieved, however, by inventing an abstract moral "nature of things," but must be worked out by examining the *de facto* constitution of some existing consciousness in which the ideals exist.

> The philosopher, therefore, who seeks to know which ideal ought to have supreme weight and which one ought to be subordinated, must trace the *ought* itself to the *de facto* constitution of some existing consciousness, *behind which, as one of the data of the universe, he as a purely ethical philosopher is unable to go. This consciousness must make the one ideal right by feeling it to be right, the other wrong by feeling it to be wrong.*[14]

Good, bad, and obligation are not absolute natures; rather, they are "objects of feeling and desire, which have no foothold or anchorage in Being, apart from the existence of actually living minds."[15]

Obligation exists in a consciousness only when there is a corresponding claim made by a concrete person. Here James enlarges the general understanding of "obligation," making *claim* and *obligation* coextensive terms, covering each other exactly. Maintaining that "every *de facto* claim creates in so far forth an obligation," he wishes to destroy the belief that "validity," which he considers an empty abstraction, has reality and gives a claim its obligatory character. He sees in the concept of validity another example of intellectualistic, extra-experiential duplication of real experience; and he asks how "such an inorganic abstract character of imperativeness, additional to the imperativeness which is in the concrete claim itself" can exist.[56]

> Take any demand, however slight, which any creature, however weak, may make. Ought it not, for its own sake, be satisfied? If not, why not. The only possible kind of proof you could adduce would be the exhibition of another creature who should make a demand that ran the other way. The only reason there can be why any phenomenon ought to exist is that such a phenomenon actually is desired. Any desire is imperative to the extent of its amount; it *makes* itself valid by the fact that it exists at all.[17]

Man's response to a concrete claim made upon him by another personal being, whether God or another human being, is certainly in no way less intelligible or less moral than a response made to an abstract, *a priori* moral order. "A claim thus livingly acknowledged is acknowledged with a solidity and fulness which no thought of an 'ideal' backing can render more complete."[18] "Wherever such [actually living] minds exist, with judgments of good and ill, and demands upon one another, there is an ethical world in its essential features. Were all other things, gods and men and starry heavens, blotted out from this universe, and were there left but one rock with two loving souls upon it, that rock would have as thoroughly moral a constitution as any possible world which the eternities and immensities could harbor."[19]

Ethics and morality exist in *persons* and among persons; goodness, evil, and obligation are humanistic phenomena. Abstract moral schemes and rules are derivative; the person and the moral features of his life are the originals of morality.

V *Moral Good and Evil*

What is moral goodness? Various goods seem to be forever in endless competition; the realization of one good often means the elimination of another:

> Various essences of good have . . . been found and proposed as bases of the ethical system. Thus, to be a mean between two extremes; to be recognized by a special intuitive faculty; to make the agent happy for the moment; to make others as well as him happy in the long run; to add to his perfection or dignity; to harm no one; to follow from reason or flow from universal law; to be in accordance with the will of God; to promote the survival of the human species on this planet,—are so many tests, each of which has been maintained by somebody to constitute the essence of all good things or actions so far as they are good."[20]

The *most universal* principle which can be discovered regarding the essential nature of good is that *the essence of good is simply to satisfy demand*. This principle, however, is of no practical value in making judgments about goodness because "demand" is such an ambiguous thing; at best, such a principle is merely a psychological insight into the moral life. The philosopher's demand for a right scale of subordination, on the other hand, is "the fruit of an altogether practical need. Some part of the ideal must be butchered, and he needs to know which part. It is a tragic situation, and no mere speculative conundrum, with which he has to deal."[21]

> Since everything which is demanded by that fact is good, must not the guiding principle for ethical philosophy (since all demands conjointly cannot be satisfied in this poor world) be simply to satisfy at all times *as many demands as we can*? That act must be the best act, accordingly, which makes for the *best whole*, in the sense of awakening the least sum of dissatisfactions. In the casuistic scale, therefore, those ideals must be written highest which *prevail at the least cost*, or by whose realization the least possible number of other ideals are destroyed.[22]

History shows the struggle from generation to generation to discover a more and more inclusive order, and in the process man has made a series of social discoveries which have made for a civilization in which a greater number of ideals may be sheltered. The laws of usages of a land are "what yield the maximum of satisfaction to the thinkers taken all together";[23] and, in cases of unresolved conflict, the philosopher must always *presume* in favor of the conventionally recognized good, until evidence dictates otherwise.

But the philosopher must never forget that ethics at any stage of history is provisional and incomplete, and must be revised day to day on the basis of experience. He also must recognize the fact that occasionally someone is born "with the right to be original," who will "replace old 'laws of nature' by better ones." He must see indeed that *applied* ethics in the old-fashioned *absolute* sense of the term is not possible because the facts needed for the construction of a moral philosophy are not all in, and particularly because metaphysical and theological beliefs are not conclusively true. Meanwhile, the good man will always seek to bring about the very largest universe of good, choosing the richer universe, voting for "the good which seems most organizable, most fit to enter into the complex combinations, most apt to be a member of a more inclusive whole."[24]

If the good man does not believe in God, he can organize his moral life in terms of other finite thinkers, who will make up his moral universe. If, on the other hand, he *does* believe in God, the perspective of his moral life will open up on to greater dimensions. When God is one of the claimants, moral life is infused with a new strenuousness. "The more imperative ideals now begin to speak with an altogether new objectivity and significance, and to utter the penetrating, shattering, tragically challenging note of appeal."[25] In a universe shared by God and man, the ethics of prudence and the satisfaction of merely finite claimants is replaced by "the ethics of infinite and mysterious obligation from on high."[26] Only in such a universe can the demands of the ethical philosopher be fully realized: "In the interests of our own ideal of systematically unified moral truth, therefore, we, as would-be philosophers, must postulate a divine thinker, and pray for the victory of the religious cause. Meanwhile, exactly what the thought of the infinite thinker may be is hidden from us even were we sure of his existence; so that our postulation of him after all serves only to let loose in us the strenuous mood."[27]

Something deep down in man tells him that there is a spirit in the universe to whom all things owe allegiance. He must see that the true significance of this life lies in its relationship to the unseen world; and he must avoid the dogmatic folly of those who say "that our inner interests can have no real connection with the forces that the hidden world may contain."[28] Indeed the highest wisdom may, paradoxically, turn out to be to give up "one's conceit or hope of being good in one's own right." Therein may lie the "door to the universe's deepest reaches."[29]

VI *The Conduct of Life*

On many concrete, specific moral questions the moral philosopher cannot say with absolute assurance what is the right answer. But the individual who must decide today what his moral obligations are cannot wait for an indefinite number of tomorrows to bring in more facts. At the present stage of knowledge, how can a man be guided towards morality? As has been seen, he will follow the laws and customs of his land in matters of a moral nature, unless he be one of those extraordinary souls by whom new moral advances come through the breaking of old laws and the substitution of more civilized ways of conduct.

In addition, he should cultivate an intelligent, effective attitude toward the existence of evil, seeing that in this world vice will always exist, with every level of culture breeding "its own peculiar brand of it as surely as one soil breeds sugar cane and another soil breeds cranberries."[30] At the same time he will see that concrete evils can be overcome. He will add his efforts to bring about the defeat of specific evils, and he will understand that *the real problem of evil is not a speculative one but one that is eminently practical.* He will not ask *why* evil should exist at all, but rather *how he can lessen the actual amount of it in this life.*[31]

A man should understand that there are no *absolute* evils and that those evils which do exist can be conquered, or reduced in their effectiveness. He should realize that *his efforts to fight evil are in line with the general drift of the universe and will be immensely strengthened by the cooperation of the universe.* His good deeds will fit in with the general nature of things, which tend to support and nourish virtue; he may hope also that his efforts will receive the active cooperation of other men and of God.

A certain modesty, however, regarding one's moral opinions is in order. A man should try to understand that he is undoubtedly insensible to many goods, probably ludicrously and peculiarly so, since even the very best of men display moral blindness in many areas. No man can hope fully to recognize and appreciate all moral goods; and no man will succeed fully in fighting for all those goods which he actively cherishes. Ignorance and failures will undoubtedly characterize most of his moral life, but these too he will philosophically accept without injury to his faith in the inch-by-inch triumph of goodness. He will see that the moral life is a war, "and the service of the highest is a sort of cosmic patriotism, which also calls for volunteers."[32] He will understand that his highest achievements will *not* be those attained in the realms of theory and speculation but the achievements reached in the realm of action and moral conduct. He will judge all things in the end by the kind of conduct which they lead to.

VII *Habits and the Moral Life*

In the development of good morals in an individual, existing forces in nature and in society should be utilized and channeled toward good actions. The biological conceptions that man is an organism for reacting on impressions and that his mind exists to help determine his reactions mean in effect that the moral development of an individual requires the acquisition of the right mass of possibilities of reaction: *"Every acquired reaction is, as a rule, either a complication grafted on a native reaction, or a substitute for a native reaction, which the same object originally tended to provoke."*[33]

The cultivation of good habits is a great ally, making the difficult easy for man by taking advantage of the "plasticity of the living matter in our nervous system. . . ."[34] From early life, as many useful actions as possible must be made automatic and habitual because, by adulthood, habits both good and bad will have inhibited or strangled most natural impulsive tendencies. In adults, possibly "nine hundred and ninety-nine thousandths of our activity is purely automatic and habitual."[35] Thus one sees that in forming habits man is shaping his future self; at any point in his life he is the imitator and copy of the self development in the past.

To form good habits, and thus *"make our nervous system our ally instead of our enemy,"*[36] James suggests three maxims: First, "take care to *launch ourselves with as strong and decided initiative as possible."*[37] "I remember long ago reading in an Austrian paper the advertisement of a certain Rudolph Somebody, who promised fifty gulden reward to any one who after that date should find him at the wine-shop of Ambrosius So-and-so. 'This I do,' the advertisement continued, 'in consequence of a promise which I have made to my wife.' With such a wife, and such an understanding of the way in which to start new habits, it would be safe to stake one's money on Rudolph's ultimate success."[38] Second, *"Never suffer an exception to occur till the new habit is securely rooted in your life."* Third, *"Seize the very first possible opportunity to act on every prompting you may experience in the direction of the habits you aspire to gain."*[39] Fourth, *"Keep the faculty of effort alive in you by a little gratuitous exercise each day."*[40]

The importance of establishing lifelong good habits becomes clear when it is understood that bad habits can make life a hell on earth, that in the making of habits men are spinning their own fates:

The Moral Life of Man

The hell to be endured hereafter, of which theology tells, is no worse than the hell we make for ourselves in this world by habitually fashioning our characters in the wrong way. Could the young but realize how soon they will become mere walking bundles of habits, they would give more heed to their conduct while in the plastic state. We are spinning our fates, good or evil, and never to be undone. Every smallest stroke of virtue or of vice leaves its never-so-little scar. The drunken Rip Van Winkle, in Jefferson's play, excuses himself for every fresh dereliction by saying, "I won't count this time!" Well, he may not count it, and a kind Heaven may not count it; but it is being counted none the less. Down among his nerve-cells and fibres the molecules are counting it, registering and storing it up to be used against him when the next temptation comes. Nothing we ever do is, in the strictest scientific literalness, wiped out.[41]

In the building up of *character*, habits, of course, play an essential part, for character is "an organized set of habits of reaction."[42] Such habits consist of "tendencies to act characteristically when certain ideas possess us, and to refrain characteristically when possessed by other ideas."[43]

VIII *Volition and Morality*

Man freely shapes the plethora of pure experience into the worlds—physical, social and psychical—in which he lives; *his drives and preferences are not mere passive products of the universe—they take active parts in humanizing and anthropomorphizing the indifferent data of experience.* Among these drives none is stronger than the desire for a world which, having moral dimensions, offers man an opportunity for *making decisions about moral good and evil and for translating those decisions into effective actions.* Human nature desires nothing less than this freedom and effectiveness; in exercising the power of building a world in terms of good and evil, man creates also the universe's greatest achievement—the morally good person.

Any deterministic philosophy, materialistic or idealistic, would, if seriously applied to life, squeeze out of existence (at least in theory) the very elements of the universe that make it most significant to man and would discredit the deepest experiences which characterize man's inner life: his feelings of responsibility and his recognition of moral goods and evils. As has been noted, deterministic philosophy created a deep spiritual crisis early in William James's life (about 1870), leading him to a "paralysis of action occasioned by a sense of moral impotence" and "the ebbing of the will to live." On February 1, 1870, James, determined to find his way back to "life," decided to acknowledge *the supremacy of morality:* "Today I about touched bottom, and perceive plainly that I must face the choice with open eyes: shall I *frankly* throw the moral business overboard, as one unsuited to my innate aptitudes, or shall I follow it, and it alone, making everything else the mere stuff for it? I will give the latter alternative a fair trial."[44]

With the alternative of "moralism" thus embraced, one may hope to conquer evil or resolve to die bravely if he fails; in either case he has been vivified by *vigor of will,* springing from a belief in its freedom. On April 30, 1870, James declared in an entry in his diary: "I think that yesterday was a crisis in my life. I finished the first part of Renouvier's second *Essais* and see no reason why his definition of free will—'the sustaining of a thought *because I choose to* when I might have other thoughts'—need be the definition of an illusion. At any rate, I will assume for the present—until next year—that it is no illusion. My first act of free will shall be to believe in free will."[45]

For James, resignation to or acquiescence in evil was impossible: "He was too sensitive to ignore evil, too moral to tolerate it, and too ardent to accept it as inevitable. Optimism was as impossible for him as pessimism. No philosophy could possibly suit him that did not candidly recognize the dubious fortunes of mankind, and encourage him as a moral individual to buckle on his armor and go forth to battle."[46]

The will, as understood in talking about good and evil conduct, involves a distinct idea of the acts to be performed and a deliberate *fiat* on the mind's part. "Such acts," James also notes, "are often characterized by hesitation, and accompanied by a feeling, altogether peculiar, of resolve, a feeling which may or may not carry with it a further feeling of effort."[47]

The will does not involve, as earlier psychologists believed, a special faculty which issues fiats that make possible all deliberate actions. All forms of consciousness—sensations, feelings,

The Moral Life of Man

and ideas themselves—tend to discharge "into some motor effect" and need no special faculty to pass over to motion, open or concealed. "The motor effect need not always be an outward stroke of behavior. It may be only an alteration of the heart-beats or breathing, or a modification in the distribution of blood, such as blushing or turning pale; or else a secretion of tears, or what not. But, in any case, it is there in some shape when any consciousness is there; and a belief as fundamental as any in modern psychology is the belief at last attained that conscious processes of any sort, conscious processes merely as such, *must* pass over into motion, open or concealed."[48]

But, fortunately, not all ideas which pass through a man's mind produce their motor consequences. In the complete field of consciousness are present an endless number of inhibiting ideas which render most ideas inoperative; nerves of arrest exert an inhibiting influence on the motor nerves. As a result, *voluntary action is "at all times a resultant of the compounding of our impulsions with our inhibitions."*[49]

In the building of character, the right volitional habits must be cultivated by providing in the mind a desirable stock of ideas and by habitually coupling the several ideas with action or inaction:

> How is it when an alternative is presented to you for choice, and you are uncertain what you ought to do? You first hesitate, and then you deliberate. And in what does your deliberation consist? It consists in trying to apperceive the case successively by a number of different ideas, which seem to fit it more or less, until you hit on one which seems to fit it exactly. If that be an idea which is a customary forerunner of action in you, which enters into one of your maxims of positive behavior, your hesitation ceases, and you act immediately. If, on the other hand, it be an idea which carries inaction as its habitual result, if it ally itself with *prohibition*, then you unhesitatingly refrain. The problem is, you see, to find the right idea or conception for the case.[50]

Even when one has found the right idea or conception for the case, it is possible that action will not follow easily or automatically. It can be that the conception is one with which the individual has formed no definite habits of action; or that the appropriate action is dangerous or difficult; or that "inaction may appear deadly cold and negative when our impulsive feeling is hot." In such cases, "we need a resolute effort of voluntary attention to drag it into the focus of the field [of consciousness], and to keep it there long enough for its associative and motor effects to be exerted."[51] "Once brought . . . in this way to the centre of the field of consciousness, and held there, the reasonable idea will exert these effects inevitably; for the laws of connection between our consciousness and our nervous system provide for the action then taking place. Our moral effort, properly so called, terminates in our holding fast to the appropriate idea."[52]

When reduced to its simplest and most elementary form, a moral act consists *"in the effort of attention by which we hold fast to an idea* which but for that effort of attention would be driven out of the mind by other psychological tendencies that are there. *To think,* in short, is the secret of will, just as it is the secret of memory."[53] *A man saves himself by thinking rightly:* a drunkard can reform only if he unwaveringly clings to correct, unflattering ideas about his vice. For all men, salvation comes, first, through their stocks of ideas; second, by "the amount of voluntary attention that they can exert in holding to the right ones, however unpalatable"; third, "by the several habits of acting definitely on these latter to which they have been successfully trained."[54]

> In all this power of voluntarily attending is the point of the whole procedure. Just as a balance turns on its knife-edge, so on it our moral destiny turns. You remember that, when we were talking of the subject of attention, we discovered how much more intermittent and brief our acts of voluntary attention are than is commonly supposed. If they were all summed together, the time that they occupy would cover an almost incredibly small portion of our lives. . . . It is not the mere size of a thing which constitutes its importance; it is its position in the organism to which it belongs. Our acts of voluntary attention, brief and fitful as they are, are nevertheless momentous and critical, determining us, as they do, to higher or lower destinies.[55]

In the development of character, *inhibition by substitution* is to be preferred to *inhibition by repression or negation.* In the case of the latter, both the inhibited idea and the inhibiting idea

The Moral Life of Man

remain in the consciousness. In the case of inhibition by substitution, the inhibiting idea "supersedes altogether the idea which it inhibits, and the latter quickly vanishes from the field."[56]

> He whose life is based upon the word "no," who tells the truth because a lie is wicked, and who has constantly to grapple with his envious and cowardly and mean propensities is in an inferior situation in every respect to what he would be if the love of truth and magnaminity positively possessed him from the outset, and he felt no inferior temptations. . . .
>
> Spinoza long ago wrote in his Ethics that anything that a man can avoid under the notion it is bad he may also avoid under the notion that something else is good. He who habitually acts *sub specie mali*, under the negative notion, the notion of the bad, is called a slave by Spinoza. To him who acts habitually under the notion of good he gives the name of freeman.[57]

CHAPTER 9

William James, Today and Tomorrow

WHEN William James died on August 26, 1910, at his summer home at Chocorua, New Hampshire, there existed no "School of William James," nor even a coherent band of disciples preaching his doctrines. It is fortunate that James's philosophy has never been structured into the doctrines of a school, for such structuring or organizing would have been a radical malformation of his thoughts.

James's thoughts *have* character and substance, but his teachings are "special" in the sense that they are not meant to be substantively *final* and fully authoritative for future thinkers. *They are starting points and suggestions for dealing with experience.* This special nature of James's philosophy invites comparison with two contemporary views of the nature of God—the traditional view of God as substance, and the rediscovered view of God as a presence to be encountered in human experience. James's philosophy is, of course, analogous to the doctrine of "encounter"; it is not totally formed; it awaits encounter with new minds and hearts.

Having studied James's philosophy, one should use it to enter into one's own experiences in truer and more adequate ways. One should attempt to understand specific experiences in terms of particular Jamesian insights and hypotheses, hoping that these experiences will respond by displaying greater intelligibility. To be a Jamesian means thus to discover high intelligibility in a variety of ever-increasing experiences: intelligibility in terms of thought, emotion, and action.

This illumination of experience by use of James's philosophic viewpoints extends to philosophic, religious, social, moral, and various other types of experiences. In religion, for example, it casts out from Christian experiences the *intellectualistic* accretions acquired from Greek philosophy and opens the way for experiences which relate truth to action, place the kingdom of God "within us," and reveal that the Sabbath was indeed made for man. In morality, the insights of William James, applied to any prevailing ethical viewpoints, cast doubt upon the *absolute* validity of "objective" codes existing prior to and independent of particular individuals. It becomes clear that, ultimately, man is not tested by such codes but that all codes are to be tested by human experiences. And socially and politically, James's belief that all structures are *man-made* opens up the challenge to remake human societies and political organizations along truly rational lines.

In one area of experience after another, James offers liberation from the closed, block-universe mentality, always calling for an open-minded, imaginative examination of many alternatives in thought and action. Thus, as an alternative to war, he suggested a moral equivalent: a war against poverty and disease. Against the entrenched orthodoxies of the medical profession, he called for freedom to approach the curing of diseases by unorthodox means. Those who would rightly understand James's philosophy must see it first of all as a means to prepare each man to deal fruitfully with his own experiences.

In many ways James's kind of thinking has entered into much of the thinking, feeling, and doing of the last half century—and with rich results. But to attempt to trace various Jamesian types of manifestations to William James's direct influence would be an intellectualistic exercise guilty of ignoring the richness of concrete reality with all of its multitudes of causes. Tracing specific literary or philosophical developments, for example, back to James would involve precisely those pedantic, arid abstractions of intellectualistic scholarship against which James battled for a lifetime.

James's influences are legitimately to be sought rather *where men are deepening their appreciation of specific concrete experiences*. In their response to these experiences they truly follow James if they show a profound awareness of the unique characteristics of the individual datum in all its manifestations —and a lively appreciation of the interactions between the individual and its total environment.

Many experiences profoundly characterized in this manner

can be found in James's own life. One such experience, rich in sensitivity, is found in a letter written in 1898 to his son Alexander, age eight. Here the philosopher recorded an extraordinary empathy with his boy and *a coyote*, an experience which presupposes a lifetime of honest and original perception:

> Darling old Cherubini,
>
> See how brave this girl and boy are in the Yosemite Valley! [Referring to an enclosed photograph.] I saw a moving sight the other morning before breakfast in a little hotel where I slept in the dusty fields. The young man of the house had shot a little wolf called a coyote in the early morning. The heroic little animal lay on the ground, with his big furry ears, and his clean white teeth, and his jolly cheerful little body, but his brave little life was gone. It made me think how brave these living things are. Here the little coyote was, without any clothes or house or books or anything, with nothing but his own naked self to pay with, and risking his life cheerfully—and losing it—just to see if he could pick up a meal near the hotel. He was doing his coyote-business, and you must do your boy-business, and I my man-business bravely too, or else we won't be worth as much as that little coyote. Your mother can find a picture of him in those green books of animals, and I want you to copy it. Your loving
>
> Dad[1]

The "influence" of William James works in the thoughts, the emotions, and the deeds of many individual men. It will grow as his viewpoints are tested and applied by various persons in their own concrete experiences. As it grows, more and more men, hopefully, will respond to the invitation to come forth *into the light of things;* and their experiences will not only be made more practically useful, but they will also be transformed by profound insights into "the nature of things":

> Instruct them how the mind of man becomes
> A thousand times more beautiful than the earth
> On which he dwells, above this frame of things . . .
> . . . .
> In beauty exalted, as it is itself
> Of quality and fabric more divine.[2]

Notes and References

Chapter One

1. Katharine (Bagg) Hastings, *William James of Albany, N. Y., (1771-1832) and His Descendants* (New York, 1924) pp. 1-6.
2. MS, Houghton Library, Harvard University.
3. James Family Papers, Houghton Library.
4. *Ibid.*
5. Anna Robeson Burr, *Alice James: Her Brothers, Her Journal* (New York, 1934), p. 11.
6. Letter (Houghton Library) to Julia A. Kellogg, December 19, 1864.
7. C. Hartley Grattan, *The Three Jameses* (New York, 1932), p. 67.
8. Letter (Houghton Library) to Julia A. Kellogg, December 19, 1864.
9. Letter (Houghton Library) to Julia A. Kellogg, June 22, [1863?].
10. Burr, p. 55.
11. Samuel M. Illsley, *New Republic* (August 22, 1928).
12. Henry James, Sr., *Literary Remains,* ed. William James (Boston, 1888) p. ii.
13. Ralph Barton Perry, *The Thought and Character of William James* (Boston, 1935) I, 130.
14. F. O. Matthiessen, *The James Family* (New York, 1948), p. 271.
15. Burr, pp. 29-31.
16. *Ibid.*, p. 45.
17. *Ibid.*, p. 131.
18. *Ibid.*, p. 85.
19. William James, *The Letters of William James,* ed. Henry James (Boston, 1920) I, 169.
20. Henry James, Jr., *Letters of Henry James* (New York, 1920), II, 43.

Chapter Two

1. Bertrand Russell, *Unpopular Essays* (New York, 1950), p. 214.
2. Alfred North Whitehead, *Dialogues* (Boston, 1954). pp. 337-38.
3. Henry James, *A Small Boy and Others* (New York, 1913), p. 8.
4. *Ibid.*, Chapters I to XIX.
5. *Ibid.*, pp. 64-67.
6. *Ibid.*, p. 74.
7. *Ibid.*, p. 44.
8. *Ibid.*, p. 68.
9. *Ibid.*, p. 234.
10. Perry, I, 59.
11. Henry James, Sr., "Autobiography," in Grattan, p. 30.
12. James, *Small Boy,* p. 207.
13. William James, *Letters,* I, 23.

14. Perry, I, 207.
15. *Ibid.*, I, 208-9.
16. William James, "Louis Agassiz," *Memories and Studies* (New York, 1912), p. 6.
17. *Ibid.*, pp. 14-15.
18. *Ibid.*, p. 5.
19. Perry, I, 216.
20. *Letters*, I, 154.
21. Hastings, p. 24.
22. *Letters*, I, 193.
23. Perry, I, 375.
24. *Letters* I, 217.
25. "The True Harvard," *Memories and Studies*, p. 348.
26. *Ibid.*, p. 350.
27. *Ibid.*, p. 353.
28. *Ibid.*, pp. 354-55.
29. William James, "What Makes Life Significant?," *The James Family*, p. 405.
30. Charles Sanders Peirce, *Collected Papers*. Edited by Charles Hartshorne and P. Weiss (Cambridge, Mass., 1934) Vol. V, #12, p. 7.
31. Perry, I, 522.
32. *Ibid.*, I, 292.
33. Charles Saunders Peirce, "A Sketch of Logical Criticism," *Collected Papers*, Vol. VI.
34. William James, *Pragmatism* (New York, 1955), p. 43.
35. *The Monist*, XV (1905), 161-81.
36. Perry, I, 654-55.
37. *Letters*, I, 169.
38. William James, *Some Problems of Philosophy* (New York, 1948), p. 165.
39. Perry, I, 659.
40. *Letters*, I, 203.
41. *Ibid.*, I, 244.
42. *Ibid.*, I, 246.
43. *Ibid.*, I, 201.
44. *Ibid.*, I, 239.
45. *Ibid.*, I, 242.
46. *Ibid.*, II, 114.
47. *Ibid.*, II, 86.
48. *Ibid.*, II, 122.
49. *Ibid.*, II, 234-35.
50. *Ibid.*, II, 290.
51. *Ibid.*, II, 179.
52. Perry, II, 508.
53. *Letters*, II, 245.
54. Perry, II, 513.
55. *Ibid.*, II, 501.
56. *Ibid.*, II, 524.
57. *Ibid.*, II, 12.

Notes and References

58. *Ibid.*, II, 11.
59. *Letters*, I, 126-27.
60. Perry, II, 11.
61. Herbert W. Schneider, *A History of American Philosophy* (New York, 1946), p. 513.
62. Perry, II, 53.
63. William James, "A Plea for Psychology as a Natural Science," *Collected Essays and Reviews* (New York, 1920), p. 327.
64. *Ibid.*, pp. 321-22.
65. Perry, II, 12-15.
66. *Ibid.*, II, 91-92.
67. *Letters*, I, 269.
68. Perry, II, 113.
69. *Ibid.*, II, 190.
70. *Ibid.*, II, 195.
71. William James, *Human Immortality* (Boston, 1899), pp. 50-52.
72. William James, "Ladd's 'Psychology: Descriptive and Explanatory,'" *Collected Essays and Reviews*, pp. 344-45.

Chapter Three

1. George Santayana, *Character and Opinion in the United States* (New York, 1955), p. 41.
2. *Ibid.*, p. 54.
3. *Ibid.*, p. 55.
4. *Letters*, I, 152-53.
5. *Ibid.*, I, 97.
6. *Some Problems*, p. 15.
7. *Letters*, II, 58-59.
8. MS (Houghton Library), "1905-6 Outline of Phil I A Course at Stanford," opp. p. 24.
9. MS (Houghton Library), "Seminar of 1903-4," pp. 74-76.
10. MS (Houghton Library), "Phil 9—1904-5."
11. "Review of *Problems of Life and Mind* by George Henry Lewes," *Collected Essays*, p. 4.
12. *Letters*, I, 190.
13. William James, *A Pluralistic Universe* (New York, 1947), p. 117.
14. *Some Problems*, p. 27.
15. Knox, *Evolution of Truth*, p. 137.
16. "Philosophical Conceptions and Practical Results," *Collected Essays*, p. 408.
17. "Chauncey Wright," *Collected Essays*, pp. 24-25.
18. *Letters*, I, 190.
19. *Ibid.*, I, 191.
20. William James, "The Sentiment of Rationality," *The Will to Believe* (New York, 1896), p. 92.
21. "Reflex Action and Theism," *The Will to Believe*, p. 125.
22. William James, *The Meaning of Truth* (New York, 1911), pp. x-xi.

23. *Pragmatism*, p. 53.
24. "Pragmatism in Italy," *Collected Essays*, p. 464.
25. Perry, II, 632.
26. "Pragmatism in Italy," *Collected Essays*, p. 465.
27. William James, *The Varieties of Religious Experience* (New York, 1903), p. 445.
28. *Ibid.*, p. 447.
29. *Ibid.*
30. *Popular Science*, January 1878.
31. *Varieties*, pp. 444-45.
32. "Philosophical Conceptions and Practical Results," *Collected Essays*, p. 410.
33. *Ibid.*, pp. 413-14.
34. *Letters*, II, 267.
35. William James, "A World of Pure Experience," *Essays in Radical Empiricism*, (New York, 1947), p. 41.
36. *Letters*, II, 203-4.
37. "Philosophical Conceptions and Practical Results," *Collected Essays*, pp. 437-38.
38. George Hodges, "William James—Leader in Philosophical Thought," *The Outlook* (February 23, 1907).
39. *Some Problems*, p. 101.
40. Walt Whitman, *Leaves of Grass, Following the Arrangement of the Edition of 1891-2* (New York, N. D.) pp. 47, 48, 39.
41. "Personal Idealism," *Collected Essays*, pp. 443-44 (italics added).
42. *Pluralistic Universe*, p. 280.
43. William James, *The Principles of Psychology* (New York, 1890), II, 617.
44. *Ibid.*, II, 624.
45. *Ibid.*, II, 619.
46. *Ibid.*, II, 620.
47. *Ibid.*, II, 625-26.
48. *Ibid.*, II, 634.
49. "The Thing and Its Relations," *Radical Empiricism*, p. 93.
50. MS (Houghton Library), "Seminar of 1903-4," p. 55.
51. MS (Houghton Library), "Article on Kant."
52. William James "Humanism and Truth," *The Meaning of Truth* (New York, 1911), pp. 61-63.
53. "Does 'Consciousness' Exist?," *Radical Empiricism*, pp. 26-27.
54. *Ibid.*, p. 37.
55. Perry, II, 366.
56. "A World of Pure Experience," *Radical Empiricism*, pp. 52-53.
57. "The Tigers in India," *The Meaning of Truth*, pp. 49-50.
58. "Does Consciousness Exist?," *Radical Empiricism*, p. 15.

Chapter Four

1. Perry, II, 632.
2. *Ibid.*, II, 631.
3. *Ibid.*, II, 549.

Notes and References

4. L. P. Jacks, "William James and His Message," *Contemporary Review* (January, 1911), pp. 23-24 (italics added).
5. *Ibid.*, p. 24.
6. *Ibid.*, p. 31.
7. Perry, II, 534.
8. *Ibid.*, II, 540.
9. *Ibid.*, II, 541.
10. *Ibid.*, II, 543-47.
11. "The Will to Believe," *Will*, p. 12.
12. *Meaning of Truth*, p. 161.
13. MS (Houghton Library), "Seminar of 1903-4," pp. 76-78.
14. *Collected Essays*, p. 43, note 1.
15. Howard Knox, *The Philosophy of William James* (New York, 1914), p. 24.
16. William James, *Talks to Teachers* (New York, 1899), pp. 23-24.
17. Knox, p. 69.
18. *Talks*, p. 26.
19. "Humanism," *Collected Essays*, pp. 449-50.
20. "Spencer's Definition of Mind," *Collected Essays*, p. 61.
21. Perry, II, 635.
22. MS (Houghton Library), "Seminary in Metaphysics 1903-4."
23. *Meaning of Truth*, p. 69.
24. *Some Problems*, p. 221.
25. "Spencer's Definition of Mind," *Collected Essays*, p. 67.
26. *Pragmatism*, p. 143.
27. Knox, p. 23.
28. "The Dilemma of Determinism," *Will to Believe*, p. 147.
29. "Reflex Action and Theism," *Will to Believe*, pp. 117-18.
30. *Pragmatism*, p. 165.
31. "Reflex Action . . .," p. 119.
32. *Pragmatism*, p. 237.
33. "Reflex Action . . .," p. 119.
34. "The Dilemma of Determinism," *The Will to Believe*, p. 147.
35. "Reflex Action . . .," p. 119.
36. *Psychology*, II, 640.
37. *Ibid.*, I, 287.
38. *Pluralistic Universe*, pp. 217-18.
39. *Some Problems*, p. 65.
40. *Meaning of Truth*, pp. 51-52.
41. *Pluralistic Universe*, p. 248.
42. "Reflex Action . . .," p. 129.
43. *Some Problems*, p. 95.
44. *Ibid.*, p. 59.
45. *Pluralistic Universe*, p. 217.
46. "The Thing in Its Relations," *Essays in Radical Empiricism*, p. 100.
47. *Some Problems*, p. 57.
48. *Ibid.*, p. 52.
49. *Ibid.*, p. 73.
50. *Ibid.*, p. 106.

51. *Ibid.*, p. 106 (italics added).
52. *Ibid.*, p. 79.
53. *Ibid.*, p. 75.
54. *Ibid.*
55. *Ibid.*, pp. 78-79 (italics added).
56. *Ibid.*, p. 79.
57. *Ibid.*, p. 80.
58. *Ibid.*, p. 81.
59. *Ibid.*, p. 85.
60. *Pluralistic Universe*, p. 60.
61. *Ibid.*, p. 68.
62. *Varieties*, p. 73.
63. Gordon Clark, *Thales to Dewey* (New York, 1957) p. 502.
64. *Letters*, II, 123.
65. Howard Knox, *The Evolution of Truth* (London, 1930), p. 139.
66. Josiah Royce, "A Word of Greeting to William James," *The Harvard Graduate's Magazine*, June 1910.
67. Andre Chaumeix, "William James, "*Revue des Deux Mondes*, October 15, 1910.
68. Perry, I, 467.
69. "Reflex Action and Theism," *Will to Believe*, p. 141.
70. "The Sentiment of Rationality," *Will*, p. 64; *Pluralistic Universe*, p. 320; "Sentiment of Rationality," *Will*, p. 79.
71. "Sentiment . . .," *Will*, p. 79.
72. *Ibid.*, p. 75.
73. *Pluralistic Universe*, p. 112.
74. "Sentiment . . .," *Will*, p. 92.
75. "Bradley or Bergson?," *Collected Essays*, p. 492.
76. Perry, II, 30.
77. *Pluralistic Universe*, pp. 112-13.

Chapter Five

1. *Meaning of Truth*, p. vi.
2. *Pragmatism*, p. 140.
3. *Meaning of Truth*, pp. vi-vii.
4. *Pragmatism*, p. 134.
5. *Meaning of Truth*, pp. v-vi.
6. *Varieties*, p. 444.
7. Knox, *Philosophy of W. James*, pp. 68-69.
8. *Psychology*, II, 321.
9. "The Will to Believe," *Will to Believe*, p. 25.
10. *Ibid.*, p. 28.
11. *Ibid.*, p. 23 (italics added).
12. *Ibid.*, p. 3.
13. *Ibid.*
14. *Ibid.*, p. 4.
15. *Ibid.*, p. 25.

Notes and References

16. *Ibid.*, pp. 26-27.
17. *Ibid.*, p. 11.
18. *Ibid.*, p. 14.
19. *Varieties*, p. 333.
20. *Ibid.*, p. 334.
21. "Humanism," *Collected Essays*, pp. 448-49.
22. "The Will to Believe," *Will to Believe*, p. 15.
23. *Pragmatism*, p. 127.
24. *Varieties*, p. 332.
25. "Will," p. 14.
26. *Psychology*, II, 617.
27. *Ibid.*, II, 661.
28. "The Moral Philosopher and Moral Life," *Will to Believe*, p. 189.
29. *Psychology*, II, 639.
30. *Ibid.*, II, 672.
31. *Ibid.*, II, 673.
32. *Ibid.*, II, 625.
33. *Ibid.*, II, 618.
34. *Ibid.*, II, 631.
35. *Ibid.*, II, 638.
36. *Ibid.*, II, 639.
37. *Ibid.*, II, 676.
38. *Ibid.*, II, 677.

Chapter Six

1. Perry, I, 471.
2. *Letters*, II, 211.
3. *Ibid.*, II, 212.
4. *Ibid.*, II, 212-15.
5. Newspaper, possibly Boston *Herald,* 1910 (Houghton Library).
6. Grattan, p. 130.
7. John Jay Chapman, *Memories and Milestones* (New York, 1915), p. 160.
8. *Ibid.*, p. 25.
9. *Ibid.*, p. 160.
10. Julius Seelye Bixler, *Religion in the Philosophy of William James,* (Boston, 1926), p. 4.
11. Knox, p. 7.
12. John Cowper Powys, *The Enjoyment of Literature* (New York, 1938), p. 36.
13. *Varieties*, p. 29.
14. *Ibid.*, p. 30.
15. *Ibid.*, p. 31.
16. *Ibid.*, p. 34.
17. *Ibid.*, p. 33.
18. *Ibid.*, p. 38.
19. *Ibid.*, pp. 41-42.
20. *Ibid.*, p. 44.
21. *Ibid.*, pp. 44-45.

22. *Ibid.*, p. 48.
23. *Ibid.*, p. 501.
24. "The Will to Believe," *Will*, p. 24.
25. *Ibid.*, p. 27.
26. *Some Problems*, p. 228.
27. "The Will . . .," *Will*, pp. 26-27.
28. *Some Problems*, pp. 223-24.
29. *Varieties*, p. 74.
30. *Ibid.*, p. 437.
31. *Ibid.*, p. 48.
32. *Ibid.*, p. 504.
33. *Ibid.*
34. "The Will . . .," *Will*, p. 23.
35. *Varieties*, p. 505.
36. Bixler, p. 84 (italics added).
37. *Ibid.*, p. 166.
38. *Varieties*, p. 144.
39. *Ibid.*, pp. 166-67.
40. *Ibid.*, p. 165.
41. *Ibid.*, p. 300.
42. *Ibid.*, p. 364.
43. *Ibid.*
44. *Ibid.*, p. 367.
45. *Ibid.*, pp. 368-69.
46. *Ibid.*, p. 424.
47. *Ibid.*, p. 73.
48. *Ibid.*, pp. 380-81.
49. *Ibid.*, p. 425.
50. *Ibid.*, pp. 420-27.
51. *Ibid.*, p. 423.
52. *Ibid.*, p. 427.
53. *Ibid.*, p. 423.
54. "Psychical Research," *Memories and Studies*, p. 204.
55. *Letters*, II, 210.
56. *Varieties*, pp. 127, 380, 379.
57. "Reflex Action and Theism," *Will to Believe*, pp. 134-36.
58. *Varieties*, p. 491.
59. *Pluralistic Universe*, p. 306.
60. Perry, I, 493.
61. "Reflex Action . . .," *Will*, p. 127.
62. *Varieties*, p. 58.
63. *Pluralistic Universe*, p. 309.
64. *Pragmatism*, p. 61.
65. *Ibid.*, pp. 61-62.
66. *Pluralistic Universe*, p. 29.
67. *Pragmatism*, p. 26.
68. *Pluralistic Universe*, p. 30.
69. *Ibid.*, p. 43.
70. *Ibid.*, p. 44.

Notes and References

71. *Ibid.*, p. 27.
72. "Reflex Action . . .," *Will*, p. 127.
73. *Varieties*, p. 525.
74. *Pluralistic Universe*, p. 44.
75. "Reflex Action . . .," *Will*, p. 122.
76. *Pluralistic Universe*, p. 124.
77. *Ibid.*, p. 318.
78. *Varieties*, p. 522.
79. *Ibid.*, pp. 447-48.
80. "Reflex Action . . .," *Will*, p. 122.
81. *Ibid.*, p. 141.
82. Perry, I, 486.
83. "The Moral Philosopher and Moral Life," *Will to Believe*, p. 196.
84. *Pragmatism*, p. 77.
85. *Varieties*, p. 517.
86. "The Moral Philosopher . . .," *Will*, pp. 213-14.
87. *Pragmatism*, p. 78.
88. *Ibid.*, p. 57.
89. *Varieties*, p. 271.
90. *Ibid.*, p. 331.
91. *Ibid.*, p. 374.
92. *Ibid.*, p. 375.
93. *Ibid.*, p. 357.

Chapter Seven

1. Grattan, p. 130.
2. Knox, pp. 97-98.
3. *Ibid.*, pp. 103-4.
4. MS (Houghton Library), "Seminary in Metaphysics, 1903-4."
5. MS (Houghton Library), "Hegelianism."
6. *Some Problems*, p. 138.
7. *Ibid.*, p. 127.
8. *Pluralistic Universe*, p. 66.
9. Perry, I, 554.
10. MS, "Hegelism" (italics added).
11. *Letters*, II, 247.
12. MS, "Hegelianism."
13. *Pluralistic Universe*, p. 325.
14. MS (Houghton Library) [F]5.
15. "On Some Hegelisms," *Will to Believe*, p. 270.
16. MS (Houghton Library), Notebook "Pure Experience (ctd)" Seminary of 1903-4.
17. *Varieties*, p. 151.
18. *Some Problems*, p. 143.
19. MS (Houghton Library), "Notes on Strong's Book."
20. *Some Problems*, p. 218.
21. "Is Life Worth Living?," *Will to Believe*, p. 62.
22. "The Dilemma of Determinism," *Will to Believe*, pp. 152-53.
23. *Some Problems*, pp. 140-41.

24. *Pluralistic Universe*, p. 351.
25. Perry, II, 748-49.
26. Perry, II, 382.
27. *Ibid.*
28. *Some Problems*, pp. 99-100.
29. Perry, II, 619.
30. *Letters*, II, 292.
31. "Is Life Worth Living?," *Will to Believe*, pp. 43-44.
32. *Varieties*, p. 501.
33. *Ibid.*, p. 474.
34. *Pluralistic Universe*, p. 185.
35. "The Will to Believe," *Will to Believe*, p. 28.
36. *Some Problems*, p. 225.
37. "The Sentiment of Rationality," *Will to Believe*, p. 101.
38. *Some Problems*, pp. 229-30.
39. *Ibid.*
40. *Ibid.*, p. 230.

Chapter Eight

1. "The Sentiment of Rationality," *Will*, p. 103.
2. "Is Life Worth Living?," *Will*, p. 61.
3. Arrian, *Discourses of Epictetus*, trans. W. A. Oldfather (Cambridge, Mass.), Book I, Chapter VI.
4. *Varieties*, p. 487.
5. *Psychology*, II, 626.
6. *Ibid.*, II, 639.
7. *Ibid.*
8. *Ibid.*, II, 661.
9. *Ibid.*
10. "The Moral Philosopher and Moral Life," *Will*, p. 185.
11. *Ibid.*, p. 189.
12. *Ibid.*, p. 191.
13. *Ibid.*
14. *Ibid.*, p. 193 (italics added).
15. *Ibid.*, p. 197.
16. *Ibid.*, p. 195.
17. *Ibid.*
18. *Ibid.*, p. 196.
19. *Ibid.*, p. 197.
20. *Ibid.*, p. 200.
21. *Ibid.*, p. 203.
22. *Ibid.*, p. 205.
23. *Ibid.*, p. 206.
24. *Ibid.*, p. 210.
25. *Ibid.*, pp. 212-13.
26. *Ibid.*, p. 213.
27. *Ibid.*, p. 214.
28. "Is Life Worth Living?," *Will*, p. 55.
29. *Pluralistic Universe*, p. 305.

Notes and References

30. Letter in Boston *Evening Transcript,* June 24, 1903.
31. *Pluralistic Universe,* p. 124.
32. *Varieties,* p. 45.
33. *Talks,* pp. 38-39.
34. *Ibid.,* p. 65.
35. *Ibid.*
36. *Ibid.,* p. 66.
37. *Ibid.,* p. 68.
38. *Ibid.*
39. *Ibid.,* p. 69.
40. *Ibid.,* p. 75.
41. *Ibid.,* pp. 77-78.
42. *Ibid.,* p. 184.
43. *Ibid.*
44. Perry, I, 322.
45. *Ibid.,* I, 323.
46. *Ibid.,* I, 324.
47. *Talks,* p. 169.
48. *Ibid.,* pp. 170-71.
49. *Ibid.,* p. 178.
50. *Ibid.,* pp. 184-85.
51. *Ibid.,* pp. 185-86.
52. *Ibid.,* pp. 186-87.
53. *Ibid.*
54. *Ibid.,* p. 188.
55. *Ibid.,* pp. 188-89.
56. *Ibid.,* p. 193.
57. *Ibid.,* pp. 194-95.

Chapter Nine

1. *Letters,* II, 81-82.
2. Wordsworth, "The Prelude," Book XIV.

Selected Bibliography

PRIMARY SOURCES

1. Writings of William James

The Principles of Psychology. 2 vols. New York: Henry Holt and Co., 1890.
Psychology, Briefer Course. New York: Henry Holt and Co., 1892.
The Will to Believe and Other Essays in Popular Philosophy. New York: Longmans, Green and Co., 1897.
Human Immortality: Two Supposed Objections to the Doctrine. Boston: Houghton, Mifflin and Company, 1899.
Talks to Teachers on Psychology, and to Students on Some of Life's Ideals. New York: Henry Holt and Co., 1899.
The Varieties of Religious Experience: A Study in Human Nature. New York: Longmans, Green, and Co., 1903.
Pragmatism, A New Name for Some Old Ways of Thinking. New York: Longmans, Green, and Co., 1907.
The Meaning of Truth; A Sequel to Pragmatism. Longmans, Green, and Co., 1909.
A Pluralistic Universe: Hibbert Lectures on the Present Situation in Philosophy. New York: Longmans, Green and Co., 1909.
Some Problems in Philosophy: A Beginning of an Introduction to Philosophy. New York: Longmans, Green and Co., 1911.
Memories and Studies. New York: Longmans, Green and Co., 1912.
Essays in Radical Empiricism. New York: Longmans, Green and Co., 1912.
Collected Essays and Reviews. Edited by R. B. PERRY. New York: Longmans, Green and Co., 1920.
The Letters of William James. 2 vols. Edited by his son HENRY JAMES. Boston: The Atlantic Monthly Press, 1920.
William James on Psychical Research. Compiled and edited by GARDNER MURPHY and ROBERT O. BALLOU. New York: The Viking Press, 1960.

2. Manuscript Materials

The Collection of James Family Papers, in The Houghton Library at Harvard University, is the greatest center for William James materials.

3. Other Primary Sources

JAMES, ALICE. *Alice James: Her Brothers, Her Journal.* Edited, with an Introduction, by ANNA ROBESON BURR. New York: Dodd, Mead and Company, Inc., 1934.
―――. *The Diary of Alice James.* Edited, with an introduction, by LEON EDEL. New York: Dodd, Mead and Company, n.d.
JAMES, HENRY (SR.). *The Literary Remains of the Late Henry James.*

Selected Bibliography

Edited, with an introduction, by WILLIAM JAMES. Boston: Houghton, Mifflin and Co., 1885.

JAMES, HENRY (JR.). *A Small Boy and Others.* New York: Charles Scribner's Sons, 1913.

―――――. *Letters of Henry James.* Edited by PERCY LUBBOCK. 2 vols. New York: Charles Scribner's Son's, 1920.

MATTHIESSEN, F. O. *The James Family: A Group Biography Together with Selections from the Writings of Henry James, Senior, William, Henry, and Alice James.* New York: Alfred A. Knopf, 1948. Contains much primary material.

MCDERMOTT, JOHN. *The Writings of William James.* New York: Random House. A large volume of selected readings, with a good original introduction.

PERRY, RALPH BARTON. *The Thought and Character of William James As Revealed in Unpublished Correspondence and Notes, Together with his Published Writings.* 2 volumes. Boston: Little, Brown and Company, 1935. A treasure house of otherwise unavailable primary material.

―――――. *Annotated Bibliography of the Writings of William James.* New York: Longmans, Green & Co., 1920; Dubuque, Iowa: W. C. Brown Reprint Library, 1964 (?). (See also McDermott, *The Writings of William James,* for updated bibliography.)

SECONDARY SOURCES

ALLEN, GAY WILSON. *William James, A Biography.* New York: The Viking Press, 1967. The only true "biography" of James.

BIXLER, JULIUS SEELYE. *Religion in the Philosophy of William James.* Boston: Marshall Jones Company, 1926. A definitive study.

BAWDEN, H. HEATH. *The Principles of Pragmatism: A Philosophical Interpretation of Experience.* Boston: Houghton Mifflin Company, 1910. Thoughtful contribution to the pragmatic-experiential philosophy.

BRENNAN, BERNARD P. *The Ethics of William James.* New York: Bookman Associates, 1961. A systematic formulation of James's moral philosophy.

BURKE, JANE REVERE. *Let Us In: A Record of Communications Believed to Have Come from William James.* New York: Dutton, 1931. A postscript on Jamesian "psychical research."

BURKLE, HOWARD R. "Toward A Christian Pragmatism," *The Christian Scholar,* XLI (December, 1958). Much still must be done to develop James's insights.

CHAPMAN, JOHN JAY. *Memories and Milestones.* New York: Moffat, 1915. Extravagant in contents and expression; defective in some judgments, but exciting—and valuable as a highly personal record.

DEWEY, JOHN. *Experience and Nature.* La Salle, Ill.: Open Court Publishing Co., 1958. Dewey explores the experience-philosophy.

EDEL, LEON. *Henry James: The Untried Years (1843-1870).* Philadelphia: J. B. Lippincott Company, 1953.

―――――. *Henry James. The Conquest of London (1870-1881).* Philadelphia: J. B. Lippincott Company, 1962.

—————. *Henry James: The Middle Years (1882-1895)*. Philadelphia: J. B. Lippincott Company, 1962. This definitive series will be completed with *Henry James: The Master (1895-1916)*, now in preparation.

GRATTAN, C. HARTLEY. *The Three Jameses*. New York: Longmans, Green and Co., 1932. Putting the Jameses in their family setting. Some harsh judgments on William.

HASTINGS, KATHERINE. *William James of Albany, New York (1771-1832) and His Descendants*. Reprinted from the *New York Genealogical and Biographical Record*, 1924. A splendid work of scholarship, thorough and richly documented.

JACKS, L. P. "William James and His Message," *Contemporary Review* (January, 1911). Jacks has a perfect understanding of James's "angle of vision."

KALLEN, H. M. (ed.). *In Commemoration of William James, 1842-1942*. New York: Columbia University Press, 1942. Essays of varying degrees of excellence.

KNOX, HOWARD V. *The Evolution of Truth*. London: Constable & Co. Ltd., 1930. Knox was a dedicated, intelligent exponent of James's philosophy.

—————. *The Philosophy of William James*. New York: Dodge Publishing Company, 1941. Brief, excellent exposition.

LOVEJOY, ARTHUR C. "The Thirteen Pragmatisms," *Journal of Philosophy*, vol. v. A classical essay.

MOORE, EDWARD CARTER. *William James*. New York: Washington Square Press, 1965. Perceptive, well-organized introduction to James's philosophy.

ROYCE, JOSIAH. *William James and other Essays on the Philosophy of Life*. New York: The Macmillan Company, 1911. Contains a brief essay on James.

SANTAYANA, GEORGE. *Character and Opinion in the United States*. New York: George Braziller, 1955. Santayana misunderstands James; shows incredible lack of perception.

WARREN, AUSTIN. *The Elder Henry James*. New York: The Macmillan Company, 1934. Excellent "life and thoughts."

YOUNG, FREDERIC H. *The Philosophy of Henry James, Sr.* New York: Bookman Associates, 1951. Comprehensive, scholarly account of the philosophy of the elder James.

Index

Absolute, the, 81, 128, 133
Absolutism, 126-28, 131
Abstraction, 27, 37, 47-48, 51, 75, 80, 82, 135, 140, 143, 146
Accidents, morphological, 95
Action, 87-88
Aesthetics, 93-94, 96
Agassiz, Louis, 24, 27, 28
Agassiz, Mrs. Louis, 31
Albany, 16, 24, 26
Antinomianism, 140
Antrim, County, 15
A priori, 56, 96-97, 144
Aristotle, 52, 68
Asceticism, 110-12
Associationist psychologies, 40

Bailieborough, 13
Barber family, 14
Ballyjamesduff, 13
Belief, 54-55, 62, 87-88, 105-8
Berkeley, George, 55
Bergson, Henri, 31, 32, 36, 37, 53, 65, 69, 70
Bible, 100
Bixler, Julius Seelye, 102, 108
"Block-Universe, The," 127
Boston, 13, 24
Bradley, F. H., 80
Brain, transmission theory of, 42-43
Brazil, 24, 28
Brown, John, 19
Buddha, Buddhism, 103, 107, 109
Burr, Anna Robeson, 16

Cambridge (Mass.), 13, 22, 23, 24, 29
Casuistry, 146-47
Catholics, 25
Causality, 131-32
Certitude, 91-97
Chance; see Tychism
Changes, 128-37
Channing, William Ellery, 109

Chapman, John Jay, 15, 101
Character, 151, 153
Charity, 125
Chaumeix, Andre, 82-83
Chemistry, 27
Chicago, University of, 37, 38, 69
Chocorua (New Hampshire), 156
Christ, 103, 125
Christian; Christianity, 96, 103, 104, 107, 109, 124, 141, 156
Christian Science, 90
Civil War, 19, 27
Claim, moral, 145-46
Clark, Gordon, 81
Classical, 34
Classification, 96-97
Columbia University, 37
Concepts, 64, 74-80
Conceptualizing, see Concepts
Concord, 19
Concrete, the, 27, 40, 49, 58, 59, 83, 157
Connections; see Relations
Connolly, Mary Ann, 14
Consciousness, 43, 50, 56, 57
Consciousness, cosmic, 112-13
Correspondence Theory of Truth, 86-87

Darwin, Charles, 68
Definition, 80
Democracy, 16, 17, 21, 133
Descartes, Rene, 56
Determinism, 34, 35, 45, 99, 126, 132, 152
Dewey, John, 37, 38, 53, 69
Dualism, 58, 60-63, 119-20
Du Bois, W. E. B., 31

Education, 50-51
Eliot, Charles William, 27
Emerson, Ralph Waldo, 15, 18, 25, 26, 36, 57, 103, 109
Epictetus, 138-39

[173]

Epicureanism, 109
Emotions; *see* Feelings
Empiricism, 35, 42, 52, 55-64, 80
Error, 64
Ethics, 93-94, 96, 102, 138-55
Europe, 24, 26, 28
Evil, existence of, 138, 144-55; problem of, 128
Evolution, 68-69, 72
Experience, 35, 49, 56-57, 58, 60-64, 66-67, 94-97
Experience, front-door (or ordinary), 141-43
Experience, house-born (or back-door), 141-44
Experience, pure, 60-64, 151
Experience, religious, 103-4

Facts, 96, 106
Feelings; passions, 84, 90, 104-8, 117
Florida, 19-20

Galileo, 42
Gifford Lectures, 98
God, 52, 53, 54, 59, 98-125, 147-49, 156-57
Goldmark, Pauline, 31
Goodness, 138, 144-55
Green, T. H., 81
Grattan, J. Hartley, 101

Habit, 149-51, 153-55
Harper's Ferry, 19
Harvard University, 23, 27, 28, 30-31, 38, 39, 100-1
Hegel; Hegelianism, 35, 38, 81, 127, 128
Heracles, 138-39
Hodgson, Shadworth, 34-35
Howison, G. H., 33
Humanism, 37, 38, 127, 140
Hume, David, 55, 59, 129
Hunt, William Morris, 26, 27

Idealism; *see* Intellectualism
Ideas, necessary, 75, 92-97
Immortality, human, 42-43
Imperialism, 23

Imperative, moral, 141-43
Inhibition, 153-55
Instrumentalism, 37
Intellectualism ("Idealism"), 36, 37, 46, 67, 71-72, 78-81, 84, 118, 126, 130, 132, 156-57

Jacks, L. P., 66
James, Alexander, 158
James, Alice, 15, 18, 20-21
James, Alice Howe Gibbens, 15, 21, 29
James, Catherine Barber, 14
James, Garth Wilkinson, 15, 18-20, 27
James, Henry, Jr., 15, 17, 18, 20, 29
James, Henry, Sr., 14, 15-18, 20, 24, 32, 33
James, Mary Robertson Walsh, 15, 16, 20
James, Robertson, 15, 18-20, 27
James, William (of Bailieborough), 13
James, William (of Albany), 13
James, William, ancestors, 13-15; angle of vision, 44-46; art studies, 26-27; career in psychology, 39-43; character, 33; colleagues, 31-39; friendships, 31-30; LL.D., 30; marriage, 29; personal religious life, 99-102; personality, 23; religious background, 25-26; teachers, 27-28
Jews, 25
Justice, 142-43

Kant, Immanuel, 28, 57, 62, 81
Kellogg, Julia A., 16
Knowledge, 42, 65-85
Knox, Howard, 37, 82, 88, 102

Language, 65-66
Locke, John, 55, 68
Longford, County, 14
Lotze, H., 92
Loyola, 109

Mahomet, 103
Materialism, 81, 130

[174]

Index

McCortney, Susan, 13
Medical profession, 28
Metaphysics, 48-49
Meliorism; *see* Universe, melioristic
Militarism, 23
Mill, John Stuart, 92, 129
Mohammedanism, 109
Monism, 34, 35, 115-16, 119, 126-37
Morality, 138-55
Morality, absolute; *see* Objectivity, ethical
Münsterberg, Hugo, 31
Mystic; mysticism, 44, 47, 99-100, 112-16

Nature, 70-71, 134-35
Negroes, 19-20, 31
Newport, 24, 27
New Hampshire, 23, 29, 156
New York, 24, 26
Nietzsche, Friedrich, 125

Objectivity, ethical, 143-44, 157
Obligation, 144-46
Optimism, 152
Option, genuine, 89
Options, living and dead, 89-90
Orange County, 14

Panpsychism, 112-13
Pantheism, 119
Papini, Giovanni, 31
Parker, Theodore, 109
Pascal, Blaise, 108
Passions; *see* Feelings
Peirce, Charles Sanders, 32, 33, 54, 75
Percepts, 64, 74-80, 131-33
Perry, Ralph Barton, 18, 41, 68, 83
Person, the human, 144-46
Pessimism, 152
Philistinism, 139
Physiology, 24, 28
Plato; Platonism, 56, 57, 65, 68, 78, 80, 96
Pluralism, 21, 34, 129-31
Poe, Edgar Allan, 18
Positivism, 32-33
Poverty, 110-12
Powys, John Cowper, 102

Pragmatism, 21, 33, 35, 36, 52-55, 65
Presbyterian, 13
Princeton Theological Seminary, 16
Psychic research, 23
Psychology, 29, 39-43
Psychology, physiological, 41

Rationalism; *see* Intellectualism
Rationality, 73, 82-85, 96-97, 113
Radical Empiricism; *see* Empiricism
Reality, 57, 65
Reason, 40, 47
Relations, disjunctive and conjunctive, 129
Religion, philosophy of, 98-125
Renouvier, Charles, 28, 34, 99, 152
Robertson, Alexander, 15
Romanticism, 83
Roosevelt, Theodore, 31
Rousseau, Jean Jacques, 44
Royce, Josiah, 31, 35, 36, 82
Russell, Bertrand, 23

Saints, 104, 107, 124-25
Salvation, 17, 135-36, 154
Sanborn, Franklin B., 19
Santayana, George, 31, 36, 44
Scepticism, 89-90, 105-8
Schiller, F. C. S., 36-38, 53
Shaler, N. S., 101
Sigwart, H., 92
Society, ideal human, 125
Socrates, 80
Soul, 41
Souls, once-born, twice-born, 109
Spencer, Herbert, 57, 122, 127, 128
Spinoza, Baruch, 35, 155
Stoicism, 104, 107, 109
Stream-of-consciousness, 42
"Strenuous Life, The," 110-11
Subjectivism; Subjectivity, 38, 65, 67, 84

Tabula rasa, 62
Theism, 118-20, 140
Thing, the, 73
Thing-in-itself, 62
Thoreau, David, 18, 23
Tillman, Elizabeth, 14

[175]

Truth, 53, 63, 67-74, 86-97, 105-8, 114-16
Truths, teleological, 68-69
Tychism, 131-34

Union College, 16
Unity, 131
Universe, 126-37
Universe, melioristic, 134-37
Universe, open, 134-36

Verification, 86-87, 91, 105-8

Walsh, Elizabeth Robertson, 15
Walsh, Hugh, 15
Walsh, James, 15
War, moral equivalents of, 110-11, 157
Waterford, County, 29
Whitehead, Alfred North, 24
"White Man's Burden," 110
Whitman, Walt, 18, 44, 58
Will, Free; *see* Determinism
Will to believe, the, 88-90, 105-8
Wilson, Katherine Van Buren, 14
Wordsworth, William, 23, 34, 158
World-consciousness, 115
World-soul, 115
Wright, Chauncey, 32
Wyman, Jeffries, 27

Kirtley Library
Columbia College
Columbia, Missouri 65216